LIFE IN A TIME OF PLAGUE

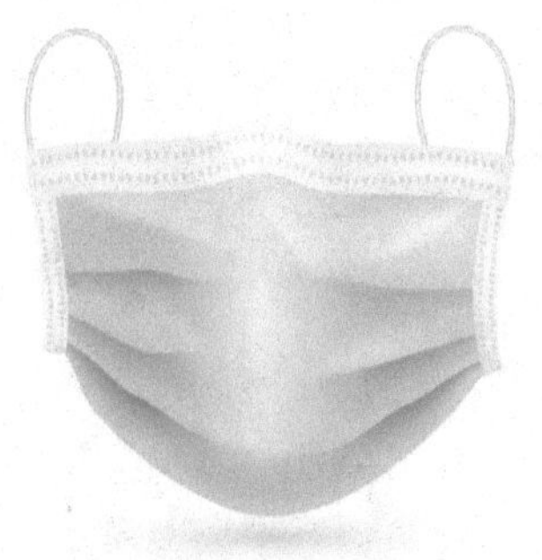

LIFE IN A TIME OF PLAGUE

A CORONAVIRUS LOCKDOWN DIARY

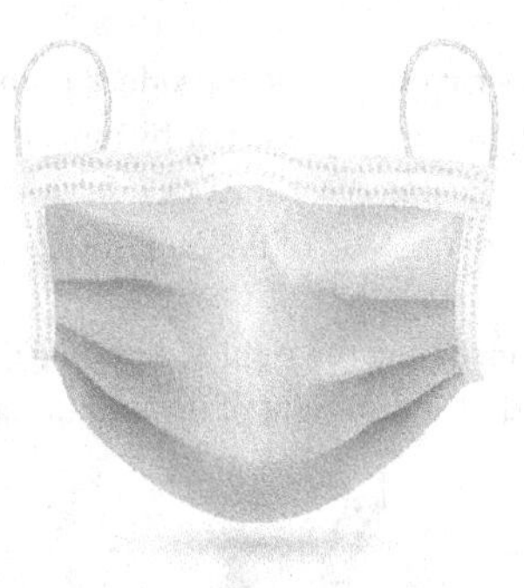

JULIAN ROUP

Foreword by Ivan Macquisten

www.blkdogpublishing.com

DEDICATION

Dedicated to all the key workers everywhere, including but not restricted to nurses, doctors, NHS hospital staff, supermarket staff, food and parcel delivery drivers, the police and the Army. You put your lives on the line to keep us going. Many of you died. We will never be able to repay your sacrifice. God bless you all.

To my sister Jay, my constant source of encouragement and wisdom, who suggested the idea for this book.

To Jan, who encouraged and edited the book daily while working, teaching online and finishing her latest novel, and who has walked beside me for four decades of marriage and 75 days of lockdown.

FOREWORD

*A plague on him dammit — why didn't I get there first? This is
the standout lockdown diary*

L ike so many others, when lockdown began, I started
writing a diary, keeping up with daily events at home,
work (I work from home anyway) and in the public
domain. I did well to keep the writing going for several weeks,
reaching around 25,000 words before work cranked up
enough again to dampen down my enthusiasm for what was
frankly becoming a chore.

My friend Julian Roup, who I first met when he was
Director of Press & Marketing at Bonhams and I was Editor
of the *Antiques Trade Gazette*, has rather better form on things
like this, already being a published author of two philosophical memoirs, *A Fisherman in the Saddle* and *Boerejood*, that strike a
chord on every page.

Now, annoyingly for the rest of us, he's done it again
by providing us with the stand-out treatise on lockdown and
what it means for him and the wider world. My small conso-
lation in being outgunned by him on the lockdown diary
front, is that I encouraged him to do it in the first place.

Life in a Time of Plague, Roup's daily diary of Covid-19
under lockdown at his secret valley home in Sussex, England,
has already been enjoying plaudits thanks to being broadcast

in a regular daily podcast and in print by BizNews in South Africa, his native land.

He describes his Sussex home as a tanker moored in the English countryside, and the diaries explore his life and feelings about the pandemic. They range far and wide, to the Cape in South Africa, and California, where his sister and brother live with their families. His age and medical issues colour this diary with a dark humour, as his age group is most at risk and the UK's NHS ride shotgun on him.

Having always thought that three score years and ten was a perfectly acceptable lifespan, he has just celebrated his 70th birthday and realised how much he wants to carry on living – as with so many of us, the restrictions on our activities that lockdown has brought have also provided us with an un-equalled opportunity to reflect on what is really important and how much we appreciate it.

I have spent lockdown reading Charles Dickens' first novel, *The Pickwick Papers*, a picaresque continuing the tradi-tion established by Fielding and Sterne.

By coincidence, BizNews reflects: "Prodigious nine-teenth century novelist Charles Dickens is known for many things, but what few know, is the one-time Parliamentary reporter was also the creator of the concept popularised by television soap operas. Dickens disrupted his industry by pub-lishing his novels as monthly serials, not complete works, starting in 1836 with *The Pickwick Papers*, published in 19 dou-ble chapter booklets over 20 months. More than a dozen more followed."

It is this tradition of the episodic deadline that has helped Roup here, as he explains:

"When I studied Journalism at Rhodes University from 1977 to 1980, I learned that journalism is the first draft of history. So with this terrible threat hanging over us, I felt that I would like to add my voice to what will become the human story of death and survival of this pandemic that has brought the world to a screeching halt.

"What has surprised me most is that amid the death, heartache and economic carnage, there is also a silver lining, a chance to simply stop and stare, and rethink our lives. I do hope that I have captured something of the essence of this time in *Life in a Time of Plague*."

Having known Julian for the best part of 20 years, I have long come to appreciate his ready wit, lilting tones and gently reflective delivery. He employs all this deftly to draw in the reader (or listener) with a charm that bewitches – but beware, because when his deeply driven liberal conscience is offended by our lords and masters, he can break that spell with a sharpness that makes you catch your breath.

Listening to him is a little like being a batsman watching the reassuring whites of a village team spin bowler as, slowly drawing back his arm, he trots up to the crease, only to discover a split second later that the stumps have gone and the umpire is directing you back to the pavilion after you've been caught by a googly.

Roup is a seriously good writer, but he's also a seriously good reader with a heft and tone that echoes the mesmerising delivery of the great Garrison Keillor. Now that the book is in print, I look forward to the audio version!

- IVAN MACQUISTEN
16TH JULY, 2020

CHAPTER 1
10th April 2020

How I almost came to a sticky end before Covid-19 could take me

These days in lockdown pass like a riffled pack of cards, each subtly different yet all much the same in shape and form. The world as we know it is turned on its head and yet the sun shines down on us endlessly in this strangest of springs.

The far-off deaths in China, Italy and Spain are now suddenly here too. For 40 years, we have lived in the English countryside in comfort and safety, observing war, famine and plague in those parts of the world subject to such things. Bizarrely, surreally, now it is our turn. And we are not ready. This sort of thing is not meant to happen here in this green and pleasant land. But the world is truly become a global village, and our distance from disaster is seen to be a thin and arrogant conceit.

I wake each day now with a sense of foreboding. Yet on reflection, I am ashamed, as I'm gifted the most precious gift of all – my life. Another day of healthy life. And I am grateful and glad of it.

Why live beyond 70, I have often thought? My body is getting creaky. I have some medical issues and arthritis is twisting my hands out of shape and making it more difficult to walk with broken knees. And yet, now that my 70th birthday approaches, with a plague death knocking at my door, a Horseman of the Apocalypse, I find myself reluctant to join the throng of refrigerated corpses the evening news shows us, wrapped in their cloths of death. I find that I very much wish to live.

I can remember clearly when it started, this lockdown, it was on the day my horse nearly killed me. I had overfed him to replace weight he'd lost after stepping on a nail and then getting colic. He was feeling his oats and kept whipping round, almost unseating me, until I lost my temper and gave him a crack with my crop. He went berserk, jumped into a ravine, hurdled a stream and galloped into dense woods. My left hand, which I instinctively used to protect my face from branches, was bleeding and felt broken. I laughed and laughed once I was able to pull up, happy to be alive.

I managed one last supermarket shop before lockdown and observed the empty shelves, the result of panic buying, the missing racks of toilet paper, the new gold. I wondered about the wisdom of crowds, and in this instance felt they were ahead of me. At the checkout, a number of items were removed from my basket and I was told that I was only allowed two each of coffee and dog food.

Each day, I sit in the garden for a time and watch spring green the trees while reading Tim Dee's *Greenery*, a gift from my sister Jay in Cape Town, and I wonder if this silent spring will be the last I see?

The skies overhead are silent at last but for birdsong. The drone of inbound flights to Gatwick and Heathrow has stopped. Higher up, the contrails of flights to every part of the world are gone for now. And in this blessed silence, the natural world is healing itself even as we die in our thousands. This is a chilling insight, a final warning, a midnight strike, of how we may end as a species, the world breathing free at last, free of this human plague.

There is a macabre black humour abroad in the world, friends and family share jokes and cartoons and comic videos over the internet. And Trump does his wicked dance of death, his plague posturing, his deceit-engraved face ever before us. And Boris making his most brilliant political move yet – coming down with the virus and in intensive care – uniting the country at last, with the good wishes of friend and foe alike. And then a mistake, emerging from intensive care on the same day as the death toll tops 1,000 – worse than the worst day in Italy or Spain.

And the medical professionals dying for lack of protective clothing. I hope fellow citizens are making a judgment, and that the day of political reckoning will not be too far off. It is Easter and this year it is Man that is now the Paschal Lamb. It is Passover, and as in times past, we pray that we will be passed over by death in these days.

I find myself abandoned by the Government which has seen fit to exclude me, one of three million self-employed, from any financial help. Big business, small businesses and salaried workers are all supported, but not me. I make a mental note to tell HMRC something of this, if I survive, next time they come seeking my tax.

I now get texts from the NHS saying they have classed me as among the most vulnerable, but if I get ill, help will not be available in hospital for me, just advice over the phone. And I am to self-isolate for 12 weeks. A classic case of don't call us, we'll call you. Die at home. This message makes me laugh out loud. But it gives me pause too. If I get ill, my wife Jan will doubtless get ill too, and how will we then cope?

Those taken into hospital with Covid-19 are not allowed family visits and those who die, die alone, with no family member by their side, just the medical professionals, who must be exhausted. So maybe a home death is preferable after all.

We are so lucky. We live in the countryside, and can exercise with ease. Jan has spent hours online and on the phone, arranging for fruit and veg, meat and bread, coffee, butter, eggs and cheese to be delivered by restaurant suppliers and those who normally supply the schools, which are now closed. Our son Dominic and his partner Stephanie top us up with everything else we may need and speak to us sternly about staying home. A strange generational shift has occurred. We the parents are the children now. They have taken on the mantle of adult responsibility for us, these two 30-year-olds. It is both a good feeling, and also an indication of the loss of independence that lies ahead if we survive.

And work continues much as before, thanks to the internet. I work from home on client business and send press releases about art and classic cars and university education to the media. There is a new camaraderie. Journalists ask how you are and wish you well and you ask about their wellbeing. I realise how good it is to work, to keep the mind occupied, to stay connected to the working world.

It is now April 10, and still the swallows have not arrived. I scan the skies, eager for the first sighting; although there are many other birds about, there is as yet no sign of that joyous, darting, swooping flight. And I breathe deep while I can, and wait.

CHAPTER 2
11th April 2020

Burnt fingers and banging pots for the NHS

Yesterday evening I made a barbecue for Jan and myself. It was a little gesture of normality, a small celebration of life, and a link to our South African heritage, a *braai*.

I used kindling and wood that has dried out over two winters – oak, ash, chestnut and silver birch – delivered by Richard Rapson, our woodsman neighbour of 40 years, who cuts our hedges each autumn with his friend and workmate, Robert Taylor. Robert surprised us last autumn with a book of his nature poetry that he self-published. Both are my age, around 70. Through the winter, Robert has climbed the 60ft to our cottage roof three times to replace wind-blown tiles lifted by the storm gales. It is not a task I would relish, and yet he charges me just £20 each time. He and his wife live in an oast house nearby, on ten acres of pastureland that delivers the bluest haze of bluebells each spring. They are about due.

I burn my fingers on the barbecue grill, being out of practice, but the food tastes good, lamb chops and Cumberland pork sausages, rice and a carrot salad. We drink wine, and it feels like a true communion with the living and our own beloved dead. Afterwards, in the gloaming, we take Gus for a walk down our lane and watch the bats winnow the air for midges and other flying insects. The sky is backlit in shell-pink, which makes the winter-bare tree branches stand out in bold black tracery. On the way home, Gus rockets down the lane, his sharp eyes having spotted deer crossing from the grass fields into the woods. He comes when I call, and we hear the deer moving fast through the woods.

Back home, we watch the TV chef Rick Stein criss-crossing his *Secret France*, hunting down those places that still offer the authentic French culinary experience, and I take mental notes to follow in his footsteps if our luck holds. We watch a film about an Orthodox Jewish woman escaping her claustrophobic marriage in New York for a new start in Berlin. And then an episode of our new discovery, *Ray Donovan*, a brutal story of a family of Boston Irish misfits transplanted to LA to wreak havoc in Hollywood. The film world portrayed is filled with more charlatans than you can shake a stick at. The death and mayhem in La La Land makes us momentarily forget what is going on all around us here in Blighty. And so to bed, after swallowing the five different kinds of pills that keep me going.

Saturday starts quietly with coffee, and a quick scan of the news and any press coverage for my clients. Then a shower and a plan for supper, having got some ideas from Jay Rayner's BBC Radio 4 *The Kitchen Cabinet*. I decide to make a simple Irish stew, but find no lamb in the freezer, so defrost some beef steaks and make beef stew based on the Italian triumvirate of caramelised onions, carrots, and celery. I add beef stock, red wine, a dash of passata, dark soy sauce, Chinese oyster sauce, salt and pepper, gluten-free flour to coat the beef, and a dash of chilli powder.

I surprise myself by making flapjacks with more of the gluten-free flour, some eggs and cream and a sachet of baking powder. They make a great breakfast served with butter and apricot jam and a second coffee. Jan and I tuck in. We are either going to roll out of here pig-fat, or each of us needing eight pall-bearers!

A neighbour, James, has kindly collected some asthma

medication for Jan at the pharmacy in town and dropped it off. No big deal normally, but now it required a special trip and the small but real chance of catching the virus in the spaced-out queue at the pharmacy.

And now, once more, I sit in the garden keeping a vigil for the swallows who must be close surely, maybe in France – Brittany or Normandy – with just the Channel to fly, exhausted no doubt from their 10,000-kilometre odyssey. Fly, friends, fly!

In the wood behind the cottage, I can hear the soft warbling of a wood pigeon, so reminiscent of the Cape turtle doves that define Africa for me.

Two nights ago, there was a strange new sound in the valley, the banging of pots with spoons to show solidarity and thanks to the frontline NHS nurses and doctors who are in the fight of their lives, for our lives and their own. It was eerie, hearing the dim echo through the trees from the town a mile away up the hill. Jan banged away with a will and smiled to hear our next-door neighbours join in.

I feel well. Though yesterday I had a slightly scratchy throat and took a slug of Jamesons whiskey, which seemed to do the job.

I listen out for news from South Africa, where my sister Jay and her husband Guy and their family live, and for news from the US, where my brother Herman and his wife Teri live with their family. The news from South Africa is good thus far, but if the virus gets into the close-packed townships, all hell will be let loose. President Cyril Ramaphosa got an early hand on things; there have been just 1,000 people infected and only one or two deaths so far. But in the US, the virus seems to be having a free run of it, and deaths there now top 20,000, even as their apology for a President mouths and gesticulates, signifying nothing. I worry for my siblings.

I find myself wondering how former work colleagues and long-lost friends are, and I reach out to them. Some reply.

On the farm next door, the endless round of work involved in caring for horses continues as usual. The young team of grooms start at 7am and finish around 5pm. They each have around eight or ten horses to feed, muck out, exercise or walk out to grass and collect later in the day. And the women who look after their own horses, around ten of them, are busy too, but with just one or two horses or ponies each. The tractor makes its endless journeys to the muckheap and back, or harrowing the grass in the paddocks to let sun and air speed the spring growth.

To our left, our neighbours Terry and Michelle and their two little boys are out in the garden with two lambs rejected by their mothers. The poor things, after the toughest start in life, have finally stopped bleating for milk. They are now working as lawnmowers, cropping the lawn and growing steadily. Terry manages the part of the farm that produces Sussex beef, lamb and wild boar, but his passion is motorbikes, and I meet him regularly in the woods on his Husqvarna scrambler.

These, then, are the sounds of this Easter, much as usual, with walkers and runners keeping their social distance, passing by in the lane from time to time.

And above us only sky. No sign or sound of aircraft, or swallows for that matter. I have faith though. They will come. I just hope I am here to see them.

CHAPTER 3
12th April 2020

A tanker moored in the Sussex countryside

Living in lockdown serves to bring one's foreground into sharp focus, and the valley we live in has never looked lovelier than in this disease-ridden spring of April of 2020.

My home valley in Sussex lies moored to its surrounding countryside like a great oil tanker, a mile long, lying east-west, its starboard and port rails, half a mile apart, fenced with hills, crowned by forest, its bow rammed hard into the fabled 'Hundred Aker Wood' of Winnie the Pooh fame at the western end of the valley.

The deck is a working landscape of farmland producing hay, as well as sheep and cattle. There is also an ever-present population of deer in herds of up to 30 animals who move in and out of the woods at dusk and dawn, feeding on the rich pasture which, after a hard winter and this unusually warm spring, has been producing grass with a 20 per cent protein count, fattening the horses that are also pastured on it for the summer.

On the southern side of the valley, the port side as it were, opposite our home on the northern, starboard ridge, there is an army camp that mostly stands empty. But now and again it plays host to men and women of the Army Reserve, the Territorials; weekend soldiers, who in days past have found themselves in Afghanistan and other theatres of war. The youngsters of the cadets are training for a role with the Territorials, and practise marching, shooting and orienteering on their weekends at the camp. They pass up and down their side of the valley and on the Forest in little groups, bearing maps, often lost, conferring among themselves and occasionally asking for directions, something that is probably against the rules. But for weeks of lockdown now, this place has been empty and silent and deer graze on the grass in front of the bungalows.

Normally, if I sit in the garden reading, if the wind is in the right direction, I can hear the sounds of drill from the camp. "Left right left right left right LEFT!" The phrase takes me back to my 19-year-old self, a conscript rifleman in the South African army, in the care of a chaotic and semi-brutal regime that owned me for nine months, and then for subsequent camps during the next eight years. It was not a happy time, and Sussex morphs in my mind's eye to the Oudtshoorn bush and the smell of *khakibos* vegetation. The feel of sweat-soaked overalls and the taste of red dust. I blink, and it's a blessed Sussex green I see again, made all the better for its new, unusual silence.

My home turf, this semi-secret green tanker floating placidly on the northern border of East Sussex and Kent, 900 feet above the sea that lies 25 miles south at Eastbourne and Brighton, is usually a peacefully busy place, producing kids for war, lambs and calves for slaughter and horses for pleasure. War, food and pleasure is our business. Death, birth and leisure. It pretty much covers the spectrum. But now death by other means has the upper hand, and food and pleasure take a back seat.

There are not many country folk around at the best of times. My neighbours, 20 in all, are scattered round the valley. Cottages grouped in ones and twos, are mostly inhabited by incomers who commute to London or Brighton, or who one way or another manage to make a living from home.

Until they moved recently there was David, a retired Colonel who keeps bees, and his wife Jane, who has a distinguished Irish literary pedigree. She is the great granddaughter of Lady Gregory, patron to the poet W.B. Yeats (who in his way brought me here, influenced as I was by his poem, Innisfree: "I will arise and go now, and go to Innisfree, And a small cabin build there, of clay and wattles made: Nine bean-rows will I have there, a hive for the honey bee"…). It remains an anthem for me, one whose ambitions I have not quite achieved. Next door to their old house lives their daughter Belinda and her husband Miles, a former lawyer who now runs a very successful recruitment business internationally. Their children, all grown up, now live away from home.

Across the valley is Ed, the former head of IT for an international company, who in retirement has returned to his first love, agriculture and gardening, and to give his full attention to the earth road to his home, which requires constant attention, or the rain will wash it away. His wife Susie is a skilled artist, whose oil paintings capture the local landscapes. We celebrated last Christmas with them, a time which now seems like a century ago, so much has happened since.

There are few really long-term residents whose families have inhabited this green haven 50 miles south of London for generations and make their living off the land. There are Richard and Robert, and Barry, who runs a wood mill and has lived on his land for years with his wife Teresa and the two children they have raised there.

Richard is a woodsman who makes a living working for local landowners, maintaining woods by planting or felling, trimming and tidying. He brings me a load of wood for £50 twice a winter, filling the back of his pick-up truck. I help him unload and stack it behind the house, under the kitchen window where it is out of the worst of the weather, which drives in on Atlantic gales from the south west, thrashing the woods like grass. His wood burns well in our New England stove that heats the living room, and the house, if sufficiently stoked up. A good place to read or dream as the horizontal rain lashes the grey stone of the house.

Richard and Robert come twice a year to cut our hedges. They take the best part of a day and leave the house with more light and neatly-edged 15-foot high beech hedges that mark the frontier of our own third of an acre of England. This place on the edge of Ashdown Forest's 6,500 acres of heather and bracken and wood has been our home this past 40 years.

Jan and I have been here so long that we are now the senior citizens hereabouts, when not so long ago we were the young newcomers. Time does play the strangest tricks.

Richard is a big, burly, slow-talking man in his fifties, a bachelor whose outfit never seems to change: a knitted hat, shirt and overalls or jeans. He is a benign presence at the cottage he calls home, half a mile down our lane, where he grows cabbages for sale at his gate, and where until a few years ago he tended to his 99-year-old blind uncle, a former farrier, with whom he shared the cottage as long as we have been here. He has never married, and seems content with his life.

At the lowest point of the valley – the bilge, you might say, if we are to continue the ship metaphor – is a hidden lake, fed by a stream that runs down from the heights of Ashdown Forest beyond, and lower down used to feed a grain mill reputed to have produced the flour for Queen Victoria's wedding cake.

Our nearest neighbour to the west of us is the farmhouse to what was once the big estate. It is a mellow stone house with a large concrete yard surrounded by stables for some 50 horses, which is today a thriving livery and jumping yard.

The biggest house in the valley was built in the Victorian era, a huge, crenulated pile used subsequently as an officers' mess for the Canadians in WWII, and since then by various colourful folk, including the singer-turned-financier Adam Faith, and John Paul Jones of Led Zeppelin. For the first 30 years of our time here, it was home to a former P&0 shipping line purser turned financier, Michael, now retired, who spoke fondly of his regular run aboard the cruise liners from Portsmouth to Cape Town each February. When the length of the English winter begins to bear down hard, he and his wife Sally take themselves off to a cottage in Hout Bay, Cape Town for a month in the sun.

Today, their house is owned by James and Camilla, who are raising a young family there. James in normal times commutes to London, where he runs one of the better-known estate agency chains.

In this valley that adopted us there is a cross-stitching, a warp and woof in the social material, that holds us together.

You cannot walk the dog without a good chat with one or two of the locals and when out riding, there are brief conversations on the network of gravel paths that crisscross the estate and the forestry plantation. Local news spreads fast. The death of a horse, a tree blocking a path, a showjumping win, the latest doings of new and old residents. Helpful local knowledge is another currency. Where the best car servicing is to be had, who provides the cheapest stable bedding, where the first English asparagus or strawberries are to be found.

Quietly, this local culture takes you in, and the sometimes harsh and always long winters are made more bearable by this local network of people who share it alongside you.

And even now, in the midst of this pandemic that has its hands to our throat, this most civil of civilities holds firm, but at a distance of two metres. And we don't chat for quite as long.

Besides our human neighbours, the valley is home also to many animal homesteaders, such as the aforementioned deer – roebuck, fallow and muntjac. There are secretive families of badgers who come out at dusk to forage, and innumerable rabbits make their homes in the artificial warrens after which the area is named: they were a medieval means of providing meat for the winter, the animals ferreted out when needed.

The local tribes of squirrels prefer their roosts in the trees and in autumn are evident everywhere, harvesting the huge weight of chestnuts. There are owls and kestrels and crows past counting, blackbirds and wrens and robins, fat wood pigeon, and each spring the swallows from Africa. And thanks to Chris and Martin, landholding neighbours who over the years have bought up the surrounding woodlands, the valley reverberates to the unearthly scream of peacocks and the rather mellower call of South American rheas, whose enclosure is half a mile from our home. The rheas and the peacocks add a touch of exoticism to this Sussex fastness.

An egg safe, just 100 feet from our front door, offers chicken, duck, turkey and goose eggs for sale with an honesty box for payment. It is a useful addition to provisioning when, as now, we are often low on supplies, and the idea of a cheese and herb omelette sounds good. At £1.20 for a box of six chicken eggs it is excellent value, and the contents fresh, with orange-yellow yolks.

And this valley is home to foxes. Their blood chilling calls sound as though some foul murder is being committed, amid screams of pain and rage. The foxes come in many shapes and sizes. Cubs in the spring, inquisitive and not yet wised up to the world, will stand and stare at you longer than an adult fox, most of whom whip themselves into the under-growth as soon as they see you.

Some though, after an insouciant glance, will merely trot off. Some are pale in colour; others have the deep lush auburn of an Irish girl fresh off the farm. Recently, I saw a dog fox so big I thought it a wolf from a distance.

In spring, the snakes emerge and the brush by the paths are home to adders, sunning themselves. We have to watch out for them in their distinctive diamond hatching of black, brown and grey, as now and then one of our cats will have a game with an adder and invariably come off worse, with a fat swollen leg where they have been bitten. A quick trip to the vet for the anti-serum does the trick, and we have not lost a cat to the adders yet.

These, then, are the denizens of the woods and fields around us. Two of the original cast are missing: wolves and wild boar. Doubtless, if you go back far enough in time there would have been others, including woolly mammoths and bears, but within man's last 1,000 years in these parts, it's just the wolves and the boar that have been hunted out. The size of the deer herds are testimony to the fact that these animals have no natural predator, with the exception of a local farrier who has shooting rights to cull a few animals each season. Deer numbers are stable, and they are under no great threat. And the wolves will not be back any time soon.

The wild boar, on the other hand, we watch and wait for, because this habitat is ideal for them. Heavy woods bearing acorns and chestnuts, grubs and insects aplenty, and a variety of farms to raid for sweetcorn and barley. Thus far, it's been a four-decade long wait for them, but they will come. A farmer to the east of us who bred them for meat has lost a few over the years, canny or strong animals who felt the call of the wild and broke out of their fenced enclosures to take up residence once more in their primordial home, the deep Sussex woods. Their spread west is best noted by panel-beating workshops that do a brisk trade in cars involved in collisions with boar. Now and then we hear stories of a farmer trapped up a haystack by a particularly belligerent animal, calling for rescue on his mobile phone to family and friends, asking for help with a shotgun.

So as we ride these woods, especially at dusk, I half keep an eye and an ear out for untoward rustlings, and note the hairs on my arm lift now and then when a shape appears to be a wild boar. Always, till now, it has been a log, or an unusual configuration of brushwood. But the day will come, sooner or later, when we will number boar among our neighbours, and then we will have to be rather more careful when walking the dog.

One of the joys of this ship-shaped valley is the fact that it is moored by the stern to a hill bearing the small town of Crowborough, out of sight among the woods and trees. But now it is mostly closed down, except for the supermarkets offering essential provisioning.

So the sense of isolation and peace one feels on board the quiet tanker floating in the woods is something of an illusion, linked as it is to all that man might need in the way of sustenance and services, including a railway station that links us to the coast and London and the wider world beyond.

It is easy enough to call for a taxi to get you from the forest farmland quiet, and within 45 minutes have you in the mad bustle of Gatwick Airport, or adding another thirty minutes to that, and depending on the London orbital M25 traffic, have you at Heathrow, one of the world's busiest airports. This is part of the joy of the deep rural quiet of this place; it has easy access to London and the world and all the sophistication and distractions it offers. But now this prized quiet spreads far and wide across England, Scotland, Wales, and Europe beyond.

It is hard to believe that such a place exists just 50 miles from one of the greatest cities in the world. A place where adders sun themselves in contentment and deer roam free to multiply at will. The sense of deep countryside increases in summer as the rampant foliage hides and disguises the sign of human habitation, trees heavy with leaf and hedgerows expanding in every direction, with Queen Anne's lace, holly, blackthorn, blackberry-briar, honeysuckle, bracken and a hundred other plant varieties.

And in the heart of the winter, as the snow falls and a deeper silence comes, it takes a good four-wheel drive vehicle to access these parts. The mile-long lane from the cottage into town is uphill for the last quarter mile, and it needs traction.

It is no surprise, then, that the town has been described as 'Scotland in Sussex' because of its weather and setting. The high Crowborough Beacon would have been visible for miles around thanks to its yellow gorse flowers, and so the origin of the name Crowborough is probably 'a golden coloured hill'.

It is attractive enough to have caught the attention of Sir Arthur Conan Doyle, the creator of the Sherlock Holmes phenomenon, who lived here for the last 26 years of his life. It is here that he wrote many of his best-known books while also serving as chairman of the local Beacon Golf Course, though an indifferent golfer himself. It is a pleasing thought that two of the most eminent Victorian men of letters, Conan Doyle and Rudyard Kipling, (based nearby at Burwash), played golf together in Crowborough. Both tragically lost sons to the carnage of World War 1, Conan Doyle finding solace in spiritualism in attempts to contact them.

Other local literary luminaries include the poet W.B. Yeats who spent some winters with Ezra Pound at Stone Cottage, Colman's Hatch, (read *Stone Cottage* by James Longenbach for more) and many summers in the early thirties with Dorothy Wellesley, at Penns in the Rocks at Lye Green, all a stone's throw from home.

To walk in the paths of these giants who wrote in part about the natural world, one instinctively knows that these miles of heath and wood entered their writing through their eyes. Another such for whom the area is famed is the creator of Winnie the Pooh, A.A. Milne, who lived over the hill on the other side of Five Hundred Acre Wood, on the outskirts of Hartfield. If this place is indeed a tanker, his home might well have been the anchor buoy.

Conan Doyle, Kipling and Milne are good company for a writer. They run the gamut from murder mystery, military and empire, to the whimsy of imagination run riot in these woods, with the stuffed animal escapees from a boy's toy cupboard. It is hardly surprising that I feel at home.

We have raised a family here, a boy and a girl, now 28 and 30; both went to London and further afield abroad to seek fame and fortune. London drew them as they grew up as insistently as iron filings are drawn to a magnet. But much as they love the excitement of the big smoke, they are also drawn to Sussex, and at present they both live nearby.

In the garden are buried cats and dogs that have been part of the family. And close by two horses, a skewbald called Traveller and Callum, the chestnut who nearly threw me, live quiet lives, munching hay. They carry us to the far corners of this world, from the tanker's deck to the surrounding seas of Ashdown Forest where after nearly four decades we are still finding new paths and hidden corners. When lockdown ends, we will once more find our way to our secret places.

At night, walking the dog, or just outside for a last commune with nature, there is another world to greet me, the constellation of stars, undimmed by city light pollution. On clear nights, they hold a comfort for me in their clarity, allowing me to get to grips with my insignificance in the scale of space and time, to realise afresh that the scourge that besets the world right now will pass, as everything does in time. There is a comfort in knowing these same stars shone down on Neanderthal man who walked this way, and will shine down on whatever is left centuries hence, when my own time here will have been as forgotten as a dream. Why this should be a comfort I do not know or question overmuch. But it is, and invariably I make my way to bed easier in my mind.

The tanker lies stilled in starlight, the hills silhouetted behind me to the north and south, west and east. All is quiet as we plough through the night, amid constellations beyond counting, in this valley I call home. And the waves of Coronavirus seems a phantom fear that we will plough through in time, and the valley will be here still, unchanged.

Chapter 4

12th April 2020

When you want to die, but can't

How can I best describe my late friend, Simone Deschamps? She was in many ways both lucky and brave. Like so many people in my life I met her through a mutual love of horses, as she stabled her black gelding Lucero at the livery yard next door to our home.

She found him in Spain, written off and due to be put down because of leg issues. She bought him anyway and nursed him back to health, and he served her well for many years in Spain and then in Sussex.

Simone was lucky for many reasons. A free spirit, she led a long, healthy life lived well in France, America, the Caribbean, Spain and England, with horses and dogs and her own skill at capturing them in paint. But finally, she was lucky for dying in her 90th year, just a month before the Coronavirus struck, killing so many residents of our nursing and old age homes. But, I suspect, she would not have minded, in fact she would probably have welcomed the virus for she was desperate to go, tired of a life without animals and constrained to one room in a care home.

When she was 78 and her horse died, she stopped riding, and then, when the last of her beautiful English Pointers died two years ago, she no longer wished to continue. But her indomitable heart was not yet ready to pack up and go. Simone tried her best to stop it herself, swallowing some forty sleeping tablets. Ruefully, she admitted to having the longest sleep of her life, some 14 hours, and waking up very much alive, but angry. Looking back, she was amused, but felt strongly that we don't manage the end of life at all well. The loss of independence and dignity, she felt, should mean an exit strategy was on offer.

Today, all across the UK, the elderly are alone with a skeleton staff in these care homes, and the residents do not have to wait long or struggle to die like Simone. The Coronavirus is having a ghastly kind of 'spring cleaning' of our most vulnerable old. It is a tragedy and a disgrace and when this horror is over, I do hope there are political consequences.

In Spain last week, the police found whole nursing homes filled with the dead, just lying in bed, their carers long fled into self-isolation. With no relatives allowed in to check how they were doing, they died alone. This horror has brought lonely deaths to so many. And we watch it all on the news, potential victims ourselves. It is no comparison but there is something of Auschwitz about this time. Each of us is metaphorically behind barbed wire, all potential victims, each day waking to the roll call of the latest dead, as the police patrol our empty streets and the charnel houses fill to bursting.

Just a month before this horror arrived, Simone died in the night of a great storm that blew some tiles off our cottage roof. When I heard in the morning that she was gone, the thought came to me that she had needed that storm to get enough wind beneath her wings. And I was glad for her. She had endlessly said that she wished to go.

Simone was an acerbic, bird-like figure, she could not have weighed 100 pounds, but she did not suffer fools gladly, and she feared nothing. Now and then I would complain of my horse misbehaving and she would shrug and say: "That is what horses do! You *want* a bit of spirit!"

She was born in France and went with her family to the US as a child of seven, when her father, a talented landscape gardener, found work on the East Coast with a wealthy landowner, whose estate gardens he designed. There Simone learned to ride and jump and race and hunt. She found work selling houses and moved to the Bahamas, where she continued in the property business. And when the Government told the expats to leave in the 1960s, she relocated to southern Spain, near Marbella. She loved the heat.

I would bump into her regularly at the stables and also as she walked her pointer down our lane in the evenings. She spoke at first in her early years in Sussex of returning to France, somewhere on the Loire Atlantic coast like La Baule, but in the end, her many friends kept her in the UK.

In her prime, she hunted with the Galway Blazers in Ireland. Now that is a statement that tells of the quality of rider she was. It is like saying about a racecar driver that he raced at Formula 1 level. And even as she crossed that fearsome bank and ditch country in the soft rain of Ireland, her keen eyes found time to observe a man in a green coat who rode across that testing country as though he was part of his horse. She always smiled at the memory. She definitely had an eye for an attractive man, although she never married. There was some talk of a pilot fiancé whose plane went down into the sea, and that was it for her.

Knowing how much she had loved hunting in Ireland, I took to reading her extracts from *The Diary of a Fox Hunting Man* by Siegfried Sassoon, and also *Some Experiences of an Irish R.M* by Edith Somerville and Violet Martin. She would sit in her favourite chair and smile a smile of pure mischief.

She was birdlike in her physical appearance, but she was no sparrow, more a sparrow hawk, and I am reminded of her each time I see a kestrel hovering above our fields, or one of the pairs of buzzards that haunt our woods or, at night, the hooting of owls. The sound of owls as they quarter the fields around our cottage always thrills me, giving as it does a sense of the tapestry of the dark being pulled back for a moment to provide a glimpse into another world.

Some of her closest friends organised a 90th birthday party for her at the care home up the lane. She got a good turnout. When Jan and I got there, the room was packed with her friends. The party table was heavily loaded with food and drink brought in by all of us who thought so much of her. Simone sat quietly, chatting now and then, a faraway smile on her face. She gave me the impression of Gatsby, not really wanting to be present at this party at all, tired out but making the best of it, trying to honour those who had come to honour her. It was a bittersweet event. And not too long after she was gone.

Simone did not want a funeral, nor anyone to attend her cremation, just a few friends to spread her ashes under a rowan tree that commanded a view of the South Downs from the heights of Ashdown Forest, where she and her dogs and horses had spent so many happy hours, and where the ashes of her dogs were sprinkled. On a cold and blustery morning, 11 of her friends gathered in the Hollies car park on the forest. Jan and I joined them, and we made our way to the rowan tree, and there her ashes blew around the base of the tree, and we knew she would be glad. Nobody spoke, just the sound of the wind, and silently we slipped away. In its way it was one of the most moving funerals I have ever attended.

She was lucky to miss the virus, which would have meant an end to all visitors for months, and she had an endless stream of them. Once she entered her bed sitting room at the residential home, she never left it, other than to go for medical appointments or to the hospital. I tried to coax her out of her room to join the other residents in the lounge upstairs, but she was having none of it. She was happy to be taken for drives or to come to tea; meals were not on, as she ate barely anything but chocolate ice cream.

I invented a Scotsman, a Mr McCracken, another resident of the home who wore a tartan waistcoat and who kept threatening to pop down to see her. She just smiled. She knew I was teasing.

What gave her the greatest pleasure was the loyalty of her many friends who filled her room with plants and flowers and sweets and magazines. And she watched horse racing right up to the end.

After spreading her ashes, we made our way off back to self-isolation, experiencing something of what Simone had, locked into our homes. But we promised each other that when this terrible time has passed, we would all gather again at the Foresters Arms in Fairwarp, to have a meal and to raise a glass to her memory.

This Easter Sunday, April 12, I wake at 7am and go downstairs to get coffee and out into the garden to look for the swallows. They are still not here. Just one fat, reckless wood pigeon, pecking at the lawn, closely watched by Gus our rescue dog, biding his time and willing the bird to come closer.

Chapter 5

12th April 2020

The first swallow of spring arrives

I saw my first swallow today, flying high and moving fast, but it was without doubt the first swallow of this spring hereabouts. Not 'ours' yet – those that nest in the stables – but an early arrival and a sign that ours are on the way. How appropriate its timing on Easter Sunday, this return of life. And how poignant, among all this death.

The great 13th century Persian poet Rumi wrote: "Beyond hopelessness there is hope." And there is hope, there has to be. Even now, especially now.

It is Nazir Afzal, Britain's former chief Prosecutor, a brilliant lawyer, speaking on BBC Radio's Today programme, who quoted these words about hope. His 73-year-old brother has just died from Coronavirus and yet he speaks of hope so powerfully in the midst of his quiet grief.

His brother had visited their 90-year-old mother in hospital in January, when she was fighting TB and pneumonia and possibly picked up the Coronavirus there. After three weeks of treatment for the virus, he was sent home to receive 'care in the community' and died in his sleep, possibly from a heart attack. The family could not find a Muslim funeral home to collect the body for burial, as they were all overwhelmed and London's morgues were full. So the family sat with the body of their dead son for 24 hours before he was collected for burial.

Nazir said that when the pandemic was beaten, lessons needed to be learned. His thirty years of public service had taught him that the rarest quality among politicians was the ability to listen. And listen now they must. Any new legislation drafted in the future, he said, required those people whose lives would be most affected by it to be central to the process of drafting any new law.

The much maligned and embattled BBC, criticised by those on the left and the right – a sure sign, if ever a sign was needed, of even-handedness – is having a good war on Coronavirus. It is often first with the news, both good and bad.

I took hope listening to our comic-turn Prime Minister on the BBC as he thanked and named the NHS nurses who had saved his life, two in particular, a female nurse, Jenny McGee from New Zealand's South Island, and Luis Pitarma, a male nurse from near Porto in Portugal, who worked tirelessly in 12-hour shifts by his side when "it could have gone either way" as Boris put it.

Ironically, both will find a future Brexit Britain that much harder to get into or stay in. A fine old irony. Maybe Boris has had a deathbed conversion to a saner course of action, but don't hold your breath.

The news from America is not good, but there is a glimmer of hope: Trump's approval ratings are falling at last. People are not buying his claim that he is not responsible for the death toll there.

Meanwhile China, it seems, is preparing to extend credit to its debtor nations, entrenching its influence and soft power. What a victory for them, inflicting this monster virus on the world and then using it to build on their power. We need to be mightily afraid of China.

Various countries and companies are racing to develop an app that will allow our smartphones to tell us if we have been in contact with someone carrying the virus. This may help to save lives now, but its implications for our future freedom is worrying.

After a quiet day, Jan and I ate a late supper and as usual, took Gus for an evening stroll in the near dark. Halfway down the lane a large owl ghosted overhead on silent wings and then curved south to scan the fields for prey. Jan took my arm and hugged it. Not hard to believe, watching it move so lightly, that its bones weigh less than its plumage.

Later, on TV, we watched a vast crowd at a 1992 Wembley tribute concert to Freddie Mercury, the vastly talented lead singer of Queen. One song stood out for good reason, that great anthem, *Who Wants to Live Forever?* Who indeed? But for now, all of us are focusing hard on surviving this horror. The concert was a reminder of that other pandemic, AIDS, which cost Freddie Mercury his life, finding him before the discovery of the anti-retroviral treatment that has saved the lives of so many.

And suddenly this morning, April 13, news on the BBC Radio's Today programme again, that a vaccine is 80 per cent ready to go and that it will be ready by September. This astonishing news comes in an interview with Professor Sarah Gilbert, an Oxford University based scientist whose clipped, authoritative delivery is as reassuring as her news, a promise of salvation. She says that clinical trials will be underway almost immediately and her own children, three adult triplets, all scientists themselves, have enrolled to take part as the first human guinea pigs. Production of the vaccine is already underway, not waiting for the end of the trial, ready to be used immediately if the trials show efficacy.

Hope after hopelessness indeed.

This morning is cold and overcast as the weather service predicted it would be, the first such weather for weeks it seems. I walk up the garden to see if 'our swallows' have arrived yet, but no. Last year's mud nests in the rafters are still empty, awaiting new life.

Chapter 6
12th April 2020

The rich man in his castle, the poor man at his gate

Our preparations for surviving the lockdown included doing a deal with others to look after our two horses, and arranging for toilet paper to be shipped in from Holland.

Jan sourced all the food and drink we might need to be delivered weekly from small Kent and Sussex suppliers that had until now been supplying schools and restaurants, as the supermarkets were overwhelmed. She ordered the loo paper from an Instagram advert one night when there was none to be had in the supermarkets, pleased that the company uses half of its profits to build toilets in developing countries. An astonishing 32 per cent of the world's population do not have safe sanitation, it pointed out.

We live on the 6,500 acres of Ashdown Forest, with a forestry plantation just behind us, so exercise is not a problem. Our son Dominic and his partner Steph come up from their boat in Brighton marina to help us with anything else we may need. Our daughter Imogen is staying with her godmother by the coast, where she helps with shopping and cooking.

In Cape Town, my sister Jay and husband Guy arranged for their housekeeper to take a paid break, and are having food delivered nightly with a recipe and all ingredients included. They live on the green belt in Constantia, so early morning walks were in order, but now the lockdown means nobody can leave their property, so that pleasure is removed. Their daughter Nikki and son-in-law Jon deliver food and other items as needed.

In Santa Barbara, California, my brother Herman and his wife Teri live on a cliff above miles of beach, so they can exercise their dogs each day as usual. Food is delivered to the door. Their daughter Lindsay and son-in-law Seth nearby can be called on in an emergency, but they cannot see them or their grandson William at close quarters.

None of this makes for hardship, yet we all speak as though we are facing an Arctic winter alone. And to be fair, death is a possibility, although when was it not?

What of the millions of poverty-stricken people living on the edge of South African cities with no toilets, or facilities for washing or showering? They are packed into corrugated iron and wood shanties like sardines. What of our own inner-city council residents here in the UK, in high rise apartments? And what of the poor across the US, mostly black and other minorities, whom statistics tell us are being hardest hit, dying in numbers totally out of proportion to their population?

Money may not buy you love, as The Beatles maintained, but it sure as hell helps to buy you life, and a comfortable one at that.

We can only wonder if this massive inequality will survive the virus's impact on our economies and lifestyles? Will we be kinder, more generous, more caring, once we've beaten the virus? My guess is maybe, for a year or two, there will be some distributive economic justice, but I fear that it won't last; we will be back to the rat race almost immediately. And why not? If this world-stopping pandemic has taught us anything, it is that money makes all the difference in surviving and doing so comfortably. Where you live and what you have in the bank can make the difference between life and death.

Another form of inequality brought into harsh focus by the pandemic is that between some men and women. There are many for whom incarceration with their significant other is the worst form of torture. It is no surprise to hear that domestic violence has more than doubled in this period – 16 women have died at their partners' hands over the past three weeks. New safe houses and refuges have been opened, and people are allowed to leave home to escape violence. Rail companies are offering free tickets to those on the run from abusive partners.

The food banks are busier than ever in this time of need. And it is a cause of national shame that in the world's fifth richest economy, people go hungry and many sleep on the streets. The homeless, however, have suddenly been housed, not so much out of compassion, but because of the fear that they might prove to be a cause of infection or further contagion.

The police are busy, struggling, as ever, to find a balance between imposing the law on aggressive idiots who cough and spit on them, and a gentler reasoning with fellow citizens who just don't get it, and keep going out for picnics and barbecues.

And life being life, love, dating and sex continue as ever, but with a new urgency, perhaps. Yesterday I read in *The Guardian* of some newly formed couples who had agreed to move in together for the duration of the lockdown. In some cases, it was working reasonably well, in others less so, as personal habits hidden during normal dating were suddenly evident in the close confines of a shared flat or room. The mystique of a new partner and the romance of new love is often not able to withstand the scrutiny of being suddenly so close up. But how to leave? The words of the song *Baby it's Cold Outside* come to mind. But it's more than cold that lies in wait beyond that closed front door.

And what of those in long-term relationships like my own 43 years with Jan. How are couples coping with the relentless, forced intimacy? The old joke about being "married for better and for worse, but not for lunch" has never seemed more relevant. In our case we tend to meet for lunch and dinner and a walk in the evening, the rest of the day taken up with writing at opposite ends of the garden, from which positions we share occasional conversation. Gus, our dog, and Saffy, our cat, shuttle backwards and forwards between us.

The constant flurry of deliveries at the front door has slowed to a stop, and the long Easter weekend has meant even fewer human contacts, not more, as work too has ended for four days. It is becoming evident that this will be a long haul, not a sprint, and that life is going to be changed for a very long time indeed.

How change will look is far from clear. There will doubtless be thousands of lost jobs as companies fold and the bounce back will doubtless take a very long time. The financial collapse of 2008 took years to rectify, and the least well off paid the highest price. But it does no good brooding on what will be; we have to get through the present, the now, that which is here that needs dealing with immediately.

Thank God for books and phones and computers and the internet, and for education, which opened up our options and our inner landscapes. Our bodies may be constrained for now, but our minds are still free to roam the earth's most remote places.

So, for now, I am choosing to fly back from Africa, tracking the swallows who have been delayed by bad weather on the way. But they are coming.

Chapter 7

13th April 2020

The pandemic landscape

To most of us without medical knowledge or, more precisely, an understanding of the behavior of epidemics, this has been a confusing time, as we grapple to understand our Government's response, and its attempt to protect us.

Slowly, however, the picture is becoming clearer. Leading immunologists give us two scenarios. The first is what happens naturally in an epidemic without medical intervention. In this case, the disease sweeps through a population killing many; hardest hit are the sick, elderly or frail – those whose immune systems are already compromised. Younger people with strong immune systems and the resilience of youth survive in greatest numbers and finally a 'herd immunity' is established.

It is interesting to be reminded by the phrase 'herd immunity' that we are, after all, just another species of animal.

This scenario poses a huge problem, especially for unprepared Governments like our own here in the UK, which has over the years run down funding for the NHS, which now is desperately short of doctors and nurses and the technical equipment needed – respirators, drugs and the personal protective clothing (PPE) that we hear so much about. Politically, the Government can't be seen to simply stand by and let nature run its course while grannies and grandpas, mothers and fathers and even children, die like flies. And it also needs to ensure that the shaky medical infrastructure is not totally overwhelmed.

Therefore we see the second scenario – an attempt to intercede in some ways to slow down the natural 'herd immunity' process. Every effort is put into 'flattening the curve' of the disease, spreading out the spike of highest deaths over a longer period to help our hospitals cope, to avoid being simply overwhelmed. That is why we get the 'lockdown' process adopted by almost every country on earth, with one or two exceptions, like Sweden. But this lockdown policy brings its own downside: the duration of the epidemic's impact is lengthened in time, and this has all sorts of human and economic costs of its own.

One of the first collateral impacts, of which we are already seeing the signs, are non-related medical impacts. People who need hospitalisation, are not going to hospital, because they are scared of getting Coronavirus there: a very real possibility. And many thousands who need attention for cancer treatment, heart treatment and other acute medical needs are not getting attention, as all medical effort is now focused on fighting one enemy and one only: Covid-19.

By the time the dust settles on this debacle, the death toll for this period and the health damage caused to the general populations will be much greater than that caused by Coronavirus deaths alone. Epidemiologists tell us that by the end of the pandemic, 80 per cent of us will have had Coronavirus – impacted mildly, almost unnoticed, or at its worst, violently and fatally. As a percentage, deaths are predicted to range from 1-3 per cent of the population, the greatest toll being among the elderly and the poor, who have little chance of self-isolation or social distancing.

Then there is the economic impact of the pandemic to national and private economies to consider. We are about to see a fall in GDP at least as great as the 6-8 per cent drop after the 2008 economic collapse and perhaps much greater; nobody at this stage has any real idea, except that it is going to be crippling. At a personal level, greater poverty will ensure that on average, all of us will live at least three months less than we might otherwise have lived.

Mental health is also being negatively impacted, and that too will have a cost that each of us will have to bear financially as taxpayers, and personally with relatives who suffer. It is a daunting prospect.

As I listen to the news and process the tidal wave of information, the Easter weekend has ended in a cold snap. The warmth of recent days is gone, and the skies overhead are grey.

What would normally have been a very busy week, with millions returning to work after the Easter break, roads and ports and airports jam-packed with bleary-eyed travellers and commuters heading back to the nine-to-five routine, is now deathly quiet. A deadly stasis hangs over us all as we cower inside our homes. Only the hospitals are hives of activity as doctors and nurses, ambulance teams, porters, cleaners and myriads of others who make up our medical infrastructure battle on night and day against this enemy.

As someone who has pronounced hermit-like tendencies, I cannot say that I have found this enforced purdah a problem. I welcome peace and quiet and am delighted to have fewer people at our front door. In recent years, I have found the increase of Amazon deliveries a growing source of irritation. But now packages are simply left in the porch, as drivers keep their distance.

Thinking and writing about my experience of this strange time, I miss my conversations with an old schoolmate and family friend, the late Professor Robert Shell. Rob, a distinguished historian whose subject was slavery and pandemics, would have been the perfect person to discuss these events with. His personal irreverence for everything was matched by a huge and forensic intelligence that he brought to his work, and his books remain essential reading for those studying his subjects.

I remember fondly his telling me of how, when at Yale, studying for his doctorate, he would make it a rule to stand while reading the *Wall Street Journal* or the *New York Times*, to focus on the essentials before his knees gave out. He was awarded his PhD in 1986, with a thesis entitled *Slavery at the Cape of Good Hope: 1680-1731*.

He is so very much missed. His uncompromising directness and honesty led to a falling out with the then South African President Thabo Mbeki, who took exception to comments Rob made about his handling of the HIV-Aids epidemic in South Africa. No doubt Rob would have had piercing insights into the current tragedy.

The news today is that both Spain and Italy are slowly, cautiously, getting back to work. In Italy, touchingly, shops selling children's clothing are among the first to be allowed to open, and in Spain it is construction and manufacturing that are going back to work.

Today I intend going for an hour-long walk in the woods, a circle walk down the back hill to the river bridge and south along the stream to the lake, crossing its retaining wall and then up the hill home. My quarry is bluebells. I will take Gus with me, and he will doubtless keep the squirrels on their toes.

Chapter 8

14th April 2020

A Covid-19 learning curve

Our learning curve on this disease is a steep one. There is news just in about a doctor, Cameron Kyle-Sidell of the Maimonides Medical Centre in New York, an emergency medicine physician at the forefront of fighting the virus, who says the behavior of the disease is not like TB or pneumonia, but much more like altitude sickness, where the lungs are fine, but are being starved of oxygen. The violence of ventilators is damaging the lungs of Covid-19 sufferers and should be used on gentler settings, he says. The cure, it seems, is killing patients. Chinese doctors have told Dr Kyle-Sidell to use oxygen himself when feeling exhausted, as you would when mountain climbing. If this proves to be true, the numbers of people surviving the illness and treatment may grow.

Meanwhile, I may have stumbled onto the reason that our swallows have not arrived. Wildlife groups in Greece say that thousands of swallows and other migratory birds have died there in the last few weeks, unable to recover from the exhausting journey from Africa, made worse this year due to strong winds and chilly weather conditions.

Scientists say that persistent strong northerly winds over the Mediterranean and the Aegean have exhausted the birds, who have been spotted in their thousands walking on streets instead of flying, as they try to recover. Photographs posted on social media show great numbers of birds lying dead in different parts of the country.

"Birds, and swallows in particular, started their migratory journey from Africa in early March, but due to the difficult weather conditions, many bird populations arrived in Greece exhausted," said Dimitris Bakaloudis, Associate Professor in the Department of Forestry and Natural Environment at Thessaloniki University.

These birds fly up to 200 miles a day, with anticyclones favouring them on their journey, lifting them higher up in the sky. They spend the winter months in the southern Sahara and as far south as South Africa and start migrating in waves from early March on a route of more than 6,000 miles.

Yesterday, as I cut the lawn for the third time this spring, I kept glancing at the sky and then to the open doors of the stables at the top of the garden, to see if I might spot that tell-tale swooping dive of the black arrows. But as the grass got shorter in green stripes, there were no birds to be seen. I moved the weathered teak picnic table and benches to a different part of the garden, closer to the kitchen, to make eating outside easier, and looked up again, but nothing.

How different things were last March in Portugal where we holidayed for ten days, soaking up sunshine after a hard English winter, coming home to a host of swallows. We were based in the Eastern Algarve town of Tavira, a lovely place with over 37 churches dotting the skyline. The tidal Gilão River runs right through it and you can watch people fishing off the bridges that cross the river. At low tide, it's not unusual to see fishermen in the shallows seeking clams on the sand bars and mud flats, watched closely by herons and egrets. There's a lovely old castle that offers great views across to the ocean and you get a good idea of the salt-making business from its heights. Tavira is filled with alleyways and small squares and restaurants serving great seafood brought in daily by local trawlers. At dusk, to sit at a riverside bar, your face tight with a day's sunshine, and sip one of the giant G&Ts on offer, as the local swallows pick insects from the river's skin, is to know happiness.

Each day, we sunned ourselves on the beaches, one in particular, Praia do Barril, reached by a footbridge over a river, and a small tourist train that took us to a mile-long beach grounded by a great rusted anchor cemetery featuring more than 100 of these giants. As usual, Jan, who is fearless when it comes to cold water, went in despite the March temperature. I preferred to warm my ageing bones on the sun loungers provided and read and doze. Now it all seems such a distant dream, but if we survive this time, maybe we will once more walk that beach and remember.

I am sure that it makes a huge difference with whom you are self-isolating. Jan and I have had our ups and downs over the four decades we've been married. Who has not? I love her and respect her deeply and admire her many good qualities. She took the lion's share of raising our children, while working full time. She is braver than me by a country mile and has an indomitable spirit. She has been known to physically intervene when someone is being attacked, once in Sicily, and once on the platform of Tunbridge Wells station, our local arrival and departure point for London. In Sicily, she punched a man in the head when he rugby-tackled her friend to the ground and tried to rape her. (He ran away). On Tunbridge Wells platform, a group of teenagers were beating up another, when Jan pulled the main attacker off the victim and gave him a piece of her mind. He was so nonplussed to be so manhandled that he and his mates took off.

A journalist like me by education and training (we met at journalism school at Rhodes University in South Africa), Jan has had a much more distinguished writing career than me. She has worked for such great names as the **BBC**, *The Guardian*, *The Observer*, the *Financial Times* and *The Spectator*, before turning to editing magazines.

Her books include *Class of 79* (Jacana Media), about three of her fellow students who were heroes of the anti-apartheid struggle, and *The World Beneath*, about a young boy growing up under apartheid (Walker Books/Penguin Random House), which was endorsed by Amnesty International and won an award for its US edition.

She works as a freelance feature writer and is currently finishing a novel and a children's book before returning to her PhD studies in September. A committed Buddhist, she chants twice a day and tells me that she mentions me in her prayers. I know that she greatly misses hosting her Buddhist meetings here, attending poetry society meetings in Tunbridge Wells and teaching creative writing as a volunteer at Share Community in London, a charity that offers a range of studies to disabled adults.

Thus far, I think, we are doing well in lockdown. I am also fortunate that my work has kept going and I am at work for part of each day for two auction clients, one selling classic cars, H&H Classics based in Warrington, and Barnebys, an auction search engine servicing some 3,000 auction houses, one of which, Julien's in Los Angeles, has just sold the manuscript of the Beatles song *Hey Jude* for almost $1m. It's a strange world, Master Jack, as another famous song puts it.

CHAPTER 9

15th April 2020

The way ahead

After another quiet day yesterday, we walked Gus down to the lake at the bottom of the hill around 5pm, to admire the early bluebells. The fluorescent green of the new growth on the chestnut trees lit our way down the sun-dappled path. We were alone in wonderland. Then a cyclist on a mountain bike came past, moving carefully downhill, one eye on Gus, whom we held onto.

Moving through this magic place, my spirits lifted noticeably. No wonder the Japanese, lovers of gardens and Zen, have a phrase for it – forest bathing. All around us, there were small vignettes of bluebells and sunlight on green and blue against the elephant-skin grey of the tree trunks, images from a children's book.

Our garden has been in lockdown itself for the long months of winter, but now old friends are re-emerging. The daffodils have been with us some weeks and now the dusky maroon Afro of the Japanese Acer is making its spring display. Year by year, it expands, forcing one to edge past it to get down the garden steps into the kitchen. It is a reminder to me continuously in summer of how little I know about plants and gardens. I planted it too close to those steps, but it is lovely, and I have no intention of moving it. If anything moves, it will have to be the steps.

In the flowerbed behind the kitchen, there are 13 huge electric pink tulips, which look so good set against the green of the newly cut lawn. They remind me of strawberry ice creams, piled to an Italian high. Above them is the real wonder of this garden, the breathtakingly beautiful Chinese Dogwood tree, which is slowly returning to life and green and which will shortly put out pink blossoms that will turn into a spectacular pinky white explosion and then, in the autumn, produce an edible reddish fruit. At its pink-white peak, it looks like a bride arriving for her wedding. Jan's childhood friend Fi, a botanist who was at the Chelsea Flower Show many years ago as designer of the South African exhibit, gave it to us, and it's been in our garden for 30 years now.

"It won't grow in South Africa," she explained. "But I've always wanted one. So I thought this was the ideal solution."

The roses are looking good too, and about to flower in May. The front of the garden is now lilac-scented, thanks to the trees in the hedge. The beech hedges around the house are turning green from their winter brown. If one has to be in lockdown, this is the perfect time.

But the world is a troubled place right now. There are voices of wisdom and voices of anger and hate in the media.

I spot an article from the author Arundhati Roy, writing in the *Financial Times:*

> "Whatever it is, Coronavirus has made the mighty kneel and brought the world to a halt like nothing else could. Our minds are still racing back and forth, longing for a return to 'normality', trying to stitch our future to our past and refusing to acknowledge the rupture. But the rupture exists. And in the midst of this terrible despair, it offers us a chance to rethink the doomsday machine we have built for ourselves. Nothing could be worse than a return to normality.
>
> Historically, pandemics have forced humans to

break with the past and imagine their world anew. This one is no different. It is a portal, a gateway between one world and the next.

We can choose to walk through it, dragging the carcasses of our prejudice and hatred, our avarice, our data banks and dead ideas, our dead rivers and smoky skies behind us. Or we can walk through lightly, with little luggage, ready to imagine another world. And ready to fight for it."

I say amen. One can only hope that mankind will listen to this wake-up call and that all the death and human suffering will not have been in vain.

My own fears about getting back to normal plague me. At my age and health, I won't survive the virus unless I have a vaccine, and that seems to be at least 18 months away. I've heard no more about the Oxford professor's work promising a vaccine by this autumn. I call my brother-in-law, Tich Walker, a retired GP in Bristol, and he says he is as unclear about the way ahead as I am. We will have to see what the Government's exit strategy is and make up our own minds on how much to put ourselves at risk, as the lockdown lifts sometime in May. Experts are saying that there could be a second, third and even fourth pulse of this virus in the months ahead. The only true safety lies in self-isolation until a vaccine is available.

There is something of the small child in me who, promised a party, wants the party. It would be wonderful to be able to celebrate my 70th on May 18 with friends and family, but I fear it is not to be.

This morning's news is led by Trump's removal of funding from the World Health Organisation because they accepted China's assurances in January that the virus was not transferable between humans. We lost six weeks to close borders, he says. I am sure that his anger is justified for once, but also know that politically he is desperate for a scapegoat, having so misled the people of the United States with his ignorance and vain assurances.

An article that gives me pause says that Ireland's death rate is 7 per 100,000 while here in the UK it is a much higher at 17 per 100,000 of population. In Ireland, the lockdown came sooner, large public gatherings banned, including St Patrick's Day, while in England, the annual festival of racing at Cheltenham, with its crowds of 250,000, was allowed to proceed, a perfect Coronavirus infection party.

And now, epidemiologists say the virus is about to sweep through sub-Saharan Africa and India. My thoughts fly south to my sister and her family there and a black woman whom I saw in a video yesterday which had gone viral. She was showing a reporter around her one-room shack outside Cape Town, where she lives with her four children and a grandson. Each part of the shack has a designated area for sleeping, cooking, bathing and chilling. She says that she does not rely on the economy, she relies on God's economy which is bountiful, and has never let her or her family down. Her face glows with joy and conviction. She is a marvel, a human diamond. Listening to her, I am humbled.

By way of contrast, fear, anger and hate stalk the world alongside the most incredible human generosity and bravery. How do the health professionals manage to put their lives and the lives of their families on the line each and every day?

I can't take too much of this dire daily dirge, so I plan supper and put two pork chops into a marinade of fresh ginger, garlic, honey, mustard, dark soy and tomato sauce. Gus shows great interest in the process. It shames me to say I've not lost my appetite, nor has Jan, nor Gus for that matter, and for now, life goes on.

CHAPTER 10

15th-16th April 2020

Spaffing Britain up the wall

Thank God for the BBC! I finish my 1,000 words for the day and switch on the radio to hear the 1pm news. After the usual depressing litany of woe, there is a repeat of the *History of the World in 100 Objects* by the former director of the British Museum, the brilliant Neil MacGregor. Today, he is speaking about Stone Age hand axes. These tools accompanied man for at least a million years, unchanged in their design. Originating in Africa's Olduvai Gorge, they came north and have been found all over Europe, the Middle East and even here in Britain, pulled out of a cliff on the Norfolk coast.

Often they are objects of great beauty as well as functionality, able to cut up a woolly mammoth or a deer. MacGregor says scientists have found that when these objects are being knapped from flint the same part of the brain used for language is activated, and so they believe that this toolmaking coincided with the start of human speech.

Some of the axes, the very beautiful ones, seem uncomfortably large to be used easily, and MacGregor wonders if they were not something of a status symbol. Powerful men co-opting art to project power in the same way we see at

Christie's and Sotheby's auctions, when a Picasso is being sold for millions.

This thought takes me back to Rhodes University in Grahamstown, South Africa, where I studied anthropology for three years and flirted briefly with the idea of becoming an anthropologist. But reason prevailed, and I became a journalist instead. During those three years, I had some contact with hand axes, and many years later at Bonhams fine art auction house in London's Bond Street, where I ran the press office, I had the privilege of holding these Stone Age axes in my hand once more and marveling at their beauty, bewitched by their vast age.

Holding such objects gave me a thrill, knowing as I did that I must be linked by family to these objects, the numbers of Australopithecines being relatively few in number. A sort of human Holy Grail, embodying food processing functionality, protection as a weapon, status symbol and art object all in one. The vast arc of time they represent also gave me an almost out of body experience while standing next to Joanna van der Lande, the Head of Antiquities at Bonhams, who showed me these miraculous stone survivals.

Sitting in the garden today, listening to Neil MacGregor speaking so eloquently about these hand axes, time collapses for a little while, and I forget lockdown and the Coronavirus. These objects also help me gain some perspective on mankind's current predicament and mine. What, after all, are a few weeks in lockdown against the span of the ages? The great accumulation of time those axes bring with them dwarfs my little life and another few weeks, or another decade, of life seem neither here nor there.

We've had another food delivery from our usual supplier and Jan has over-ordered on the pickles, not realising they are restaurant size! We now have enough dill pickle gherkins in two huge jars, each a foot and a half tall, to keep a Jewish deli in business for at least a month. I wonder what a slice would be like with a G&T?

The postman delivered a letter from the NHS today, offering sympathy for my being stuck at home for 12 weeks and suggesting ways of keeping amused, reading, listening to music and cooking being some of the suggestions. They have also just texted me to say I should expect a telephone call checking up on me to see if I have all that I need. The trouble-making side of my nature wonders what would happen if I asked for a full body massage when they call? (They never do).

Listening to the news once more, the lacklustre Health Minister, Matt Hancock, who looks sicker by the day, was finally, reluctantly, promising the social care sector some help with personal protective clothing (PPE). Thousands of sick and elderly citizens are dying in their care homes, and the staff who are trying to help them are exhausted and at their wits' end.

When this shit-show is over, and Britain is found to lead Europe, possibly the world, with its death toll, I do hope that Boris's recent comment is recalled, that spending police budgets on child abuse claims is 'spaffing money up the wall'. (Spaff is slang for ejaculate, and I have to presume here Johnson means the money spent on child abuse claims would be wasted). Let's hope his self-image as Britain's new Churchill is remembered for the sick joke it is, as he has certainly 'spaffed' Britain up against the wall with his half-arsed response to the Coronavirus. How many thousands of the dead would be alive today if we had a competent Prime Minister; our would-be 'King of the World' – as he told his sister Rachel was his ambition as a child – is another sad, deluded little Trump-lite.

There is a further depressing descant to this song of destruction echoing across Britain – news of the scammers who are using the disaster to line their own pockets. People selling fake masks or just pretending to, others shipping cocaine in under medical supplies, and many others who don't miss an opportunity to kick us when we are down. If we are at war, these people are traitors and saboteurs who should suffer the same fate as if this was a shooting war. Is that too much to hope for? I am so often angry just now.

Helping my mood and preventing me going on a killing spree of my own are the hundreds of yachting vlogs I have watched during this time and before it too. Thanks to these vlogs from so many, especially the two that got me into this watching spree in the first place, the remarkable couple on La Vagabonde (the team who sailed the climate protestor Greta Thunberg and her father across the Atlantic to Lisbon), and SV Delos, which has been going round the world for a decade with two brothers who had not sailed previously and suddenly decided to run off to sea. Remarkable people all, whose courage, fortitude, inventiveness and great good humour in the face of sometimes overwhelming weather is humbling. Free Range Sailing is another favourite, a young couple who are hugely knowledgeable about living off the sea and the land.

This morning, I found a new one that did something truly remarkable: it dropped 50 years off my age and made me feel 20 again. Four young American surfer-sailors, led by a grizzled Frenchman, took a Gunboat Catamaran named Vela from Hawaii to the Lion Islands 1,000 miles to the south, at a very respectable pace. It is so charged with male energy and goodwill and esprit de corps, that I longed to be 20 again and full of vigour, thrilled by the world and all that it offered.

At one point on the journey, Vela is moving slowly in very light airs, and the lads leap in for a swim. There is a wonderful underwater image of one of the crew hanging onto the rudder boards, pulled along horizontally in the deep blue. It is the absolute image of an undersea angel flying through the sea.

Thanks to these videos, I am regularly at sea rather than in my rickety steamer chair in the garden. They have taken me vicariously – minus seasickness – across every ocean on earth, to the Arctic and Antarctic, the cruising grounds of the Caribbean, the Mediterranean and Thailand. I've circumnavigated the world with SV Delos and watched families form on RAN, Delos and La Vagabonde. Thanks guys, you've all been lifesavers.

As I look down the lawn, there is a path sprinkled with daisies where my footsteps to the horse's feed room through the winter has compacted the soil, encouraging this blossoming in the grass; a floral snowdrift that commemorates my morning and evening strides across the green. A spoor of flowers. *Los net 'n spoor* they say in Africa. Just leave a trail. With this writing, I am doing my best.

CHAPTER 11

17th April 2020

Another three weeks

I wake up to find 25 deer in the field opposite the cottage, heads down, grazing contentedly. The lockdown has been extended for another three weeks, and the peace this Friday is tangible. A thought comes to me, that I have had increasingly these past few weeks – I'm going to miss this time when it's over. Why? The reasons are numerous. I enjoy the quiet, the sense that the whole world is stopped momentarily from its mad rat-race to destruction. I like the fact that though my work has almost dried up, demands for payment from various bodies have also stopped, as few people are at work. This gear shift is good, and as the old saying goes, a change is as good as a holiday.

There are so many fewer demands on my time, just cooking and walking the dog, not onerous tasks. There has been a devastating cost for many in lost loved ones and economic hardship, but personally, I would be happy to see this time extended if we could just put a stop to the dying and the financial concerns for everyone.

This morning's news is led by a much-needed happy story. A 99-year-old WWII army veteran, Captain Tom Moore, set out to raise £1,000 by walking 100 laps of his garden before his 100th birthday, using his walking frame for support. To his astonishment, the country has donated £15m (and at the time of recording this, a month later, it is £30m) and now the great British public is demanding he get a knighthood. Ah, Blighty.

The *Financial Times* today reports that the UK is setting itself apart from the rest of the world by maintaining loose border controls, even as dozens of countries continue to clamp down on international travellers, in an attempt to stem the Coronavirus outbreak. As the number of infections worldwide rose above two million this week, Britain remained in a small club of nations that have failed to match the tighter borders and stringent quarantine rules on arriving travellers that are now common in other countries. "The UK is an outlier," said Professor Gabriel Scally, president of epidemiology and public health at the Royal Society of Medicine. "It is very hard to understand why it persists in having this open-borders policy. It is most peculiar." More than 130 countries have introduced some form of travel restrictions since the Coronavirus outbreak began, say Oxford University researchers tracking the measures. These include screening, quarantine and bans on travel from high-risk areas. But not Britain. WTF?

News that both China and the US are lifting their lockdowns in a phased way is making the news. China has adjusted its death toll figure in Wuhan up to 3,000 and says its economy fell by 6.5 per cent. Nobody believes anything that comes out of Beijing, so who knows. The same goes for the idiot in the White House.

After our 1½ hour long walk in the woods yesterday, Jan and I have good appetites and for supper I make grilled chicken and a salad. On our walk, we passed two other couples with their dogs, two horse riders from the yard next door, and a rather dodgy looking tattooed man in a singlet coming across the wall of the lake.

At present, British walking etiquette is more pronounced than ever; people try their best to avoid coming close, and one or two stick to the truly unique British custom of simply not seeing you. They walk past, ignoring any greeting, eyes to the fore. Even after 40 years here I find it strange and irritating. Is it shyness, social awkwardness, annoyance that anyone else shares their space, a desperate need for privacy on a small crowded island? Or a mixture of all these things? I have never really understood it or come to grips with it. And, if anything, when I'm out horse riding, it's worse. I might be forgiven for thinking I was invisible.

After supper, Harriet Doherty pops in after horse riding locally, collecting more clothes for our daughter Imogen who is in lockdown with her and her mother Julia over near Rye in Kent. Hattie hovers at the garden gate, while we stay by the cottage's storm porch. I have not seen her for a decade at least, not since she was around 18, and we catch up briefly. This is a girl we have watched grow up, as her mother is Imogen's godmother and Jan's close friend. Hattie looks so much like a younger version of her mother, who, like her, is an accomplished artist. I have no doubt that Hattie's work will make her name in time. My years at Bonhams and consultancy for other art auction houses and galleries has honed my eye a bit and Harriet definitely has talent. She looks like a 1940s Land Army girl in her breeches and windcheater, splashed with mud. She has a very old-fashioned English beauty, blond and rose, and she radiates good will, intelligence and competence. We are sorry to see her go.

When she leaves, with the clothes and the food and wine Jan has added to her load, including one of the oversized jars of pickles that we know Imogen loves, we watch a 1993 film on Sky, *Carlito's Way*, with Hollywood stars Al Pacino and Sean Penn. Pacino is a gangster who tries to go straight after leaving prison but is sucked back into crime by everyone he knows including Penn, his lawyer. The evening flies by. For Hollywood, it seems crime does pay.

During the day, I received a telephone call from a friend, Martin van der Zeeuw in Holland, and I speak to my brother in California.

Martin tells me that the Dutch are pretty much going about their business as usual, despite lockdown and social distancing. He lives next to the spectacular tulip fields of Kuikenhof outside Amsterdam, which my mother said were surely a foretaste of heaven after she visited them. Martin says that the millions of tourists who visit each year have not arrived and the blooms have been cut three weeks early. He is a classic car journalist and editor and has an encyclopaedic knowledge of cars. Last year, he survived a triple heart bypass and is once again cycling, driving and working. When I had my stents inserted, he was very kind and supportive. We have a kind of survivors' club, the third member being Tich, my brother-in-law in Bristol, who suffers from arrhythmia. At present, all three of us crocks are well. But God help us if we catch this virus.

In Santa Barbara, my brother Herman and wife Teri are missing their grandson William, aged three, whose language skills have blossomed in lockdown. Sadly, William believes that he is being punished by his parents by not being allowed to see his friends. It must be so difficult to explain to a child his age what is going on without frightening them.

Our niece Nikki and her husband Jon are in lockdown in Cape Town with two bright, energetic, demanding daughters Sophia 11, and Abi, 8, who they are homeschooling.

To help them cope, Jon has come up with a brilliant wheeze to use up some of the girls' endless energy. Their ankles are tied to an elasticised rope harness in the swimming pool where they can use every muscle swimming strongly, but not actually going anywhere. They will probably emerge with shoulders like rugby forwards and be able to swim the English Channel with ease. They also have a tent in the garden to give them a sense of camping and to give them some distance from the adults.

Lockdown with kids is not for sissies.

Chapter 12

17-18th April 2020

Food looms large in lockdown

We decide to drive to a part of Five Hundred Acre Wood and walk down to inspect the place where my horse Callum almost did for me. But my car won't start. The battery on my CLS Mercedes is dead as a doornail. I will have to jumpstart it later and let it charge for a while. So Jan drives us out to the Forest, where Gus is delighted with the new territory and all its exciting smells.

We have the place to ourselves, and its green incandescent trees shadowed with the emerging bluebells and the prehistoric fronds of bracken unfurling like the prow of Viking longships. In the deep woods, we stop and listen to the sound of the wind in the treetops; not a breath reaches the ground, where it is utterly still. We keep a lookout for the resident buzzards, but they are absent. The day before, we saw one, down the hill from the cottage, doing circuits overhead, searching for prey. They have made serious inroads into the local snake population, and I can't say I'm sorry that there are fewer adders around. I'm not a fan of snakes, and in the past we've had to rush cats and dogs to the vet for a shot against snakebite when paws have swollen up badly after a bite. Now it is the lizards that are doing well, says Terry, our next door neighbour who looks after the farm. And the rabbits are coming back strongly too this year, he says.

After about a mile, we get to the spot where Callum and I both lost our tempers, and the evidence is still clearly visible on the ground in hoofmarks in the clay this side of the river and among the heavy leafmould on the far bank, where his mighty leap took us. If ever one needed proof of his jumping pedigree, here it was. Both his sire and dam jumped internationally for Ireland and Germany. But Callum's had an easy life with his first owners, who have pootled him around English farms and countryside, the reason his legs are in such good nick.

Showing Jan the spot, and inspecting the area, I see a heavy low branch that we must have dodged, just too low for Callum to fit under, and I see the marks where he sidestepped it with a swerve. Had we hit that, I doubt I would be writing this.

Each day we keep a lookout for the swallows, but still nothing. With the author of *Greenery*, Tim Dee, I am currently keeping watch vicariously on the Rock of Gibraltar for birds on the western Mediterranean Flyway, returning from Africa. I am amazed by what passes him, flying low and flying high, and his intricate knowledge of the birds' physical appearance, feeding habits, preferred home turf, winter and summer.

On my laptop this morning, I watch Tom Cunliffe, one of the greatest British sailors of his generation, speak about crossing the Atlantic in September back in 1973 with his wife, too late in the season to be wise. The Atlantic took its toll on them and their 70-year-old 32ft pilot cutter, which had no engine, nor any of today's modern navigational tools, mobile phone, satellite iridium phone, radar, GPS, AIS, nor anything much in the way of technology. They were forced to hove-to and mend a smashed tiller, which had pulled free from the rudder when waves "greybeards higher than the mast" tossed them around like a matchstick. He is currently in Coronavirus lockdown with his wife too, and doing talks to the yachting fraternity. It is a happy time for them, he says, much like being at sea, reading, writing and cooking.

Speaking of cooking, my sister Jay, who is no mean cook, emails as if she is reading my mind, something I think she is more than capable of: "Tonight it is masala ostrich meatballs on cabbage and roasted sweet potatoes." Yum. Don't think I've ever eaten ostrich. It does seem a terrible sadness to hear of these majestic birds ending up as meatballs. But that would not stop me trying the dish and doubtless finding it delicious. The ostrich is one of my totem animals, ever since on the day I finally finished my national service army training in Oudtshoorn, back in 1969, and pulled the car over onto the hard gravel shoulder to watch one of the most astonishing spectacles I've ever seen – ostriches in that desperately dry countryside dancing in the rain, wings outstretched. An image of joy, if ever I've seen one. I can remember crying for joy myself.

I'm going to walk down shortly to check on Callum in his field, as he is barefoot for the first time since I've had him, almost a year now, as I'm not riding. Hopefully a month hence, I will get Matt, the farrier, to put his virtually unused set of shoes back on again and start riding. My waistline could do with the exercise. Thank God we can still walk.

Jan sends me a worrying cutting about food riots in South Africa and the police and army deployed to prevent this and other criminal activity during lockdown. The writer Abdul Kariem Matthews warns that if law-abiding folk start looting to enable them to eat to survive, there will be meltdown. He attaches a photograph of some black graffiti painted onto a white wall which reads: "Corona is the virus, Capitalism (heavily underlined) is the pandemic."

Boris is still recuperating at Chequers, the PM's country residence. The medical community are understandably at their wits' end about a shortage, or rather a total lack of personal protective clothing. The BBC reports an hour ago that 'Half of humanity is under social distancing curbs.' What a sobering thought.

As world Coronavirus deaths pass 150,000, more than 4.5 billion people are under containment to slow the pandemic. Germany has just seen four days of increasing death tolls.

Doctors in Japan say some hospitals are struggling to cope with the influx of patients, even turning ambulances away.

The UK death toll reached 14,576 on Friday as 847 new deaths were reported in hospitals, but these figures do not include the dead in nursing homes and retirement homes, nor those who've died at home. President Trump said US lockdown protesters were being treated 'rough' after calling for the 'liberation' of some states. The WHO advised countries to plot a cautious path out of lockdown, rather than relying on antibody tests.

I have a major concern myself; I'm out of marmalade. This is no small thing, as my day starts with coffee then an hour later a second cup with buttered toast and marmalade, one of the great loves of my life. I've even written about it for *Country Life* magazine. Jan promises to see if she can get some delivered, maybe in a catering size, like the bloody great jars of gherkins. That might be enough.

In Praise of Marmalade begins: "In the lemon light of an English morning, the orange marmalade glows like a church window with the compressed heat of a Spanish summer. In that jar of jellied fruit live a thousand memories of breakfast-in-bed mornings, of sunlight on a woven cream counterpane, of silence, and the rustle of pages turning; of your sun-kissed skin, your copper hair. It is a fragment of time, bitter sweet, like the shards of orange peel encased in amber.

"Marmalade, it is an English passion – just how they like it, bottled and kept beneath a lid for safety – a quiet secret indulgence, enjoyed early, with the rest of the day in which to recover. It is a passion I share, in this at least we are alike, my no longer new compatriots and I."

I will need marmalade to survive lockdown!

CHAPTER 13

19th April 2020

A sleepwalking Britain

Now and then I will cough or sneeze, and a little tremor of foreboding runs through me. Last thing at night, just before going to sleep, and first thing in the morning when waking up, I check my breathing and lung capacity and breathe more easily once I feel that all is well. And I say a little prayer of thanks.

The official death toll stands at 15,500 today but there are the uncounted 4,000 dead in nursing homes, an under-reported number, and then there are the home deaths, so the true figure must be around 20,000 dead at least from Coronavirus on April 19.

It is a beautiful Sunday morning, and *The Observer* reports: "Humanity will have to live with the threat of Coronavirus 'for the foreseeable future' and adapt accordingly, because there is no guarantee that a vaccine can be successfully developed, one of the world's leading experts on the disease has warned. This stark message was delivered by David Nabarro, professor of global health at Imperial College, and an envoy for the World Health Organisation, on Covid-19, as the number of UK hospital deaths from the virus passed 15,000."

Other nations were quick out of the blocks on this catastrophe and with the use of testing, tracing, isolation and lockdown, minimised deaths. Britain, still arguing about Brexit and a new Tory landslide Government elected just before Christmas, celebrating its victory, has sleep-walked into this horror. And there is not going to be any 'All Clear' siren ringing out over the land anytime soon. The spectre of death is going to be haunting us for a very long time. We will get up with it and go to bed with it and it will be an unwelcome guest at every human contact we have, however far away from each other we stand.

A very significant political development this morning comes in the form of a devastating front-page blast in the *Sunday Times*, owned by Rupert Murdoch, Britain's media kingmaker whose ring every would-be Prime Minister is expected to kiss. It describes how "over the past 38 days, Britain has sleep-walked into catastrophe," making mistake after mistake. Having Murdoch turn on them in this savage way will electrify the Tories. Coronavirus is making for strange bedfellows. I never expected to find Murdoch in my bed. Go figure!

For most of us, the economic results are going to be devastating at a personal level as well as at a national level. And in the end, because of the threat of impoverishment, we are going to have to accept the higher death rate of our elderly, rather than bankruptcy and social destabilisation. We've reached a point that many so called 'simple societies', hunter-gatherers like the San Bushmen, reach with old and sick relatives – they are left behind, propped up against a tree or under a bush with an ostrich egg full of water, to await death as the young and fit march on.

There are strange and exquisitely horrible stories emerging from the mess. Police are calling for an end to 'lockdown-shaming' as a weapon in feuds. Police forces are receiving thousands of complaints about lockdown rule-breaking and they fear many of these are being used to settle scores. Britain is a nation now using the Coronavirus to continue fights with neighbours. The vendetta has arrived. So much for the Spirit of the Blitz.

In the US, Black and Latino communities are the hardest hit by the virus. In New York, which has become the global epicentre of the disaster, black men are nervous about wearing masks, as this has traditionally made them targets for the police.

Meanwhile, Trump criticises state governors for 'going too far' with the lockdown, as he gives support to those who are protesting against it across Middle America.

And for those of us cheered up by the music industry and its antics, this morning brings reviews of the One World At Home Concert with among others, Madonna, Lady Gaga, Elton John, Billie Eilish and The Rolling Stones, singing from their living rooms in isolation. The voyeur in me is as interested in the furnishings as the artists and their songs.

The UK's open borders policy – suddenly so different from its Brexit closed borders policy – is leading to some bizarre results. Our approach is turning Britain into a refuge for the richest travellers. "We've seen a very big increase in the number of super yachts coming to the UK to berth because they cannot enter ports in the Mediterranean," said Anne Carson, owner of Super Yacht Services Falmouth. "I would say there have been 20 or more in the last few weeks alone, which is very high for this time of year."

Anything to do with the spending power of these people, or just Christian goodwill? We will never know.

And to be fair – cease my cynical heart – at least 15,000 people are still flying in to the UK each day with no screening for Coronavirus, according to Matt Hancock, the Health Secretary, not all of them billionaires surely? Hancock (increasingly referred to as Matt Handjob) said the equivalent of 105,000 travellers land per week, including from hotspot nations such as China, Italy and the United States. The Government has not imposed any health checks or quarantine periods for people coming into the country. In contrast, the US banned all travellers from Europe, and New Zealand enforced a mandatory 14-day quarantine for anyone entering.

The UK Government has consistently said screening passengers on arrival here would do very little to contain the spread of the virus. During an appearance on Good Morning Britain earlier this week, Mr Hancock defended the position. He said: "We don't test at airports because the number of people coming through has dropped dramatically. The epidemiological impact of keeping travel open is very small because there's already large transmissions here." Testing also often fails to identify sufferers due to the virus's two-week incubation period.

The airports are also open to facilitate the entry of cargo including food, and to allow for the repatriation of UK citizens stranded abroad.

The Financial Times reports: "The UK is setting itself apart from the rest of the world by maintaining loose border controls even as dozens of countries continue to clamp down on international travellers in an attempt to stem the Coronavirus outbreak. At two million this week, Britain remained in a small club of nations that have failed to match the tighter borders and stringent quarantine rules on arriving travellers that are now common in other countries. "The UK is an outlier," said Professor Gabriel Scally, president of epidemiology and public health at the Royal Society of Medicine. "It is very hard to understand why it persists in having this open borders policy. It is most peculiar."

More than 130 countries have introduced some form of travel restrictions since the Coronavirus outbreak began, say Oxford University researchers tracking the measures. These include screening, quarantine and bans on travel from high-risk areas. As a result, at least 90 per cent of the global population lives in countries with restrictions on non-citizens and non-residents arriving from abroad, while 39 per cent live behind borders that are entirely closed to foreigners, according to analysis published at the start of April by the US-based Pew Research Center. Since then, authorities in Japan, China, Germany and elsewhere have tightened or extended travel controls, while many require arriving passengers to be tested.

Heaven help us – Michael Gove MP is chairing the group running the UK, while Boris recovers. The group includes Richie Sunak the Chancellor and Dominic Raab, the Foreign Secretary. Not that the return of Boris to Number 10 gives me any greater confidence of good Government, just more pratfalls.

Here at home, yellow warning signs that say 'Stay Home' have gone up in the woods nailed to trees. This is a consequence of so many more walkers than usual using the woods, and some of them criticising horse riders who are also using the woods to exercise their animals.

To take my mind off all the trouble of the world yesterday, I baked a loaf of wholemeal bread as Jan has finally managed to source some dry yeast, which like flour, has become as rare as gold dust. It is delicious, if I say so myself, and as she is wheat-intolerant, I have it all to myself! When cool, I slice it up and place it in the deep freeze for use as toast. I am filled with the energy of a homesteader, a survivor.

As I eat my breakfast on the lawn this morning, I can hear our neighbours' children playing with the two orphan lambs, who now follow them around like pet dogs. The family dogs, Roo and Belle, are somewhat bewildered by this turn of events.

At times my husbandly patience runs thin indoors. Jan asks me to use antiseptic spray on the taps before I turn them off after washing my hands, on the food as soon as it is delivered, on the front door handle, on my phone daily, on my clothes when I've carried a box of food into the kitchen. She's right of course, but I have to suppress irritation each time she does it. I have to remind myself that this virus is deadly in its infectiousness and Jan is simply trying to protect me, to save my miserable life. Grudgingly, I comply. How stupid is that! Next door, on our left, I can hear a dressage competition starting up. As I believe horses to be the best medicine, I can hardly take umbrage, but it does drive home the fact that currently, following Government advice, I am not riding, nor is Jan.

As I finish typing, I look up to see swallows flying circuits of our garden and then perching on the TV aerial on the cottage roof. *Our swallows are back from Africa!* At least I've lived to see that this spring. I can feel tears welling up. Thank God for small mercies.

CHAPTER 14

20th April 2020

We spring a leak and so does the UK Government

Make no mistake: despite the spring weather, we are in the middle of a storm. The total death toll in Europe, excluding Russia, has passed 100,000, according to Johns Hopkins Coronavirus Resource Center. The global death toll has reached 162,070.

But there are small mercies in among this dire news. I realise how lucky we have been that Boris came down with the virus. Imagine what the death toll would have been had he been well? Between celebrating his election victory, threatening the EU with a no-deal-Brexit, going on holiday to the Caribbean and giving the Cobra Meetings a miss for five weeks as the solids started to hit the fan, he has been an absentee landlord, and probably just as well. Things could well have been worse, no doubt, had he been properly in charge.

On the home front, we've sprung a leak from our water meter in the garden. I report it to Anglian Water and Claudia promises an inspection visit soon. I wonder how many days it will take, and am astonished to get a call from an inspector an hour later who says he is parked out in front of the cottage and is looking at the problem for us. How amazing is that! I am humbled by people like this, ordinary people going about their work keeping the country's infra-structure going. I thank him profusely.

As trouble never comes singly, Jan announces that our 20-year-old dryer has finally bitten the dust and orders a rotary outdoor dryer which she says will save money on electricity. Let's hope the sun continues to shine.

I get stuck into some work for a client, H&H Classics, who will shortly be selling four vehicles found abandoned in a Derbyshire field for 35 years, which will be sold on April 29 in an online auction. Each of the two cars and two trucks will need years of loving restoration, which will cost a fortune. I am always amazed by the passion the classic car collecting fraternity have for these old crocks, which they restore to *concours d'élégance* condition, with no expense spared.

I walk down to check on Callum, whom I find at the far end of his paddock. As I come up to pat him, he gives me a good nip on my right arm, as if to say: "I haven't forgotten the arm that whacked me!" Getting him back into work may prove interesting, when it comes.

This morning, *The Guardian* reports that disabled people are being left without food, after being missed off the Government's list of those vulnerable to Coronavirus.

The Government set up an online register billed as a way to reach 'extremely vulnerable' households in England who have been told to shield for 12 weeks – either offering them food parcels via their local authority, or liaising with major supermarkets to give priority for online delivery. But now it has emerged that large numbers of disabled and older people are being excluded from the scheme, due to the highly selective criteria.

One hundred people with severe disabilities and chronic illness say they have been rejected for the Government's register and thereby left without any support to access food without leaving their home, despite being particularly vulnerable to Coronavirus.

Their conditions include cancer being treated with chemotherapy, heart disease, tetraplegia, motor neurone disease (MND), myalgic encephalo myelitis (ME) and muscular dystrophy. Some disabled people reported sleeping to avoid hunger pains, or living off fruit. At least one rejected for assistance has gone on to contract Coronavirus.

"I've had four letters to say I should be shielding, yet the Gov UK site doesn't recognise me to be put on the online vulnerable list," said 40-year-old Vicky McDermott in Northumberland, who has the immune disorder rheumatoid arthritis and a daughter with a life-limiting condition, who has also been told to shield.

"I tried registering last night for the fifth time. The supermarkets won't put us on the priority list, as we're not registered with the Government."

But both doctors and patients report confusion over how this is being handled. When Denise Stephens, 41, who has multiple sclerosis and is immuno-compromised, was rejected, she followed instructions to call her GP but hit a brick wall. "My GP said they couldn't help me and they didn't know why the Government is directing people to them about this," she said. Last month, Stephens contracted Coronavirus. She has had to call an ambulance twice to her London home, but is still not eligible for help with food or medication.

The charity WellChild estimates many of the 100,000 children and young people with serious medical conditions in the UK do not meet the criteria for the extremely vulnerable list.

There are also concerns that the Government is excluding people whose disability means they cannot physically distance safely at supermarkets, such as those with sight loss or autism. One woman with autism and mental health problems, who is self-isolating, said she had lost her carer, who helped her shop, but still did not make the vulnerable list. "I'm absolutely terrified I'll be dying of starvation in the coming weeks," she said.

Happily, the Government is facing increasingly rigorous scrutiny of its actions in several areas over its preparations for and response to Coronavirus. Thus far the main areas of criticism are:

DEATH RATES

The most obvious and tragic crisis of all. The UK has now recorded more than 16,000 Coronavirus-related deaths in hospitals, and thousands more are believed to have occurred in care homes and elsewhere. This puts the UK on an apparent course to match the very high death rate of places like Italy. The Government is, however, urging caution over direct comparisons, given the different ways in which statistics are collected across nations, time lags in terms of the outbreak, and demographic differences. At Sunday's Downing Street briefing, the deputy chief medical officer for England, Jenny Harries, said a meaningful comparison might not be possible until some months after the pandemic had eased. Why am I not surprised?

TESTING

The UK remains very low down the international league table for the proportion of the national population tested for the virus, a measure seen as crucial to tracking its spread and thus laying the ground for a gradual end to the lockdown. The Government has already missed its target of 25,000 tests a day by mid-April, and remains some way short of its end-of-April goal of 100,000 a day; 21,626 were carried out on Saturday. There is also no sign of the promised millions of simpler antibody tests, as their accuracy remains dubious, even though the Government bought 3.5m of one type.

PPE

The lack of PPE has proved to be one of the most difficult tasks for the Government – getting enough PPE to not just hospitals, but also care homes and other settings like prisons and local authorities. On Friday, it emerged that guidance had changed to say NHS staff should use smaller, less effective aprons if, as seemed imminent, stocks of full gowns ran out – troubling news for hospital workers amid growing numbers of staff deaths.

A consignment of gowns was due to arrive as part of a shipment of PPE from Turkey on Sunday, but has been delayed. Ministers have pointedly declined to guarantee supplies as needed, saying the situation is very challenging, given the massive global demand for supplies. In the meantime, staff have to decide whether to agree to work without proper protection.

VENTILATORS

On the one hand, despite initial fears, there has not yet been a massive shortage of the complex machines used to help people breathe as they try to fight the virus and to help their lungs recover, but even after the UK's target to secure 30,000 was downgraded to 18,000, that figure has still not been met. However, there has been political fallout over the apparent confusion about a plan to get private companies to design and build new models.

HOSPITAL CAPACITY

As with ventilators, while there was initial panic at the idea of critical care beds being quickly overwhelmed, this has not been the case. The temporary acquisition of private spaces and the rapid construction of new sites has seen the number of these beds rise from about 4,100 in February to more than 5,500 now, with the occupancy rate falling from 81 per cent to 58 per cent. However, the overall numbers of beds remain below what was pledged.

POLITICAL LEADERSHIP

This might be the big one in terms of future focus. While Boris Johnson's long absence due to Coronavirus is bad luck, the news that he missed five meetings of the Government's emergency committee while taking a break from No 10 when the virus was first emerging in the UK has prompted condemnation. His ministers insist that Johnson remained in charge.

Why is it, I wonder that Britain is once again a nation of lions, led by donkeys? This phrase, popularly used to describe the British infantry of the First World War and to blame the generals who led them, seems relevant again. If one replaces soldiers with NHS staff, the comment holds up to scrutiny.

Chapter 15

21st April 2020

Life or money?

It is a fine old irony that Britain is waiting today for an 84-ton delivery of personal protective equipment being flown in from Turkey. I recall that huge billboard image of refugees 'massing on our border' that helped the rightwing mafia to swing the Brexit debate in their favour, among the other tricks they got up to, using misinformation in ways that Goebbels would have appreciated. The image of foreigners hammering on our gates elicited a near panic to close the UK borders as soon as possible, before millions of 'free-loading Turks' descended on us as soon as they achieved EU membership. A complete nonsense and fabrication. The news picture agency, Getty, confirmed its photographer took the image of refugees in Slovenia, in 2015, and the billboard, created for Leave.EU, was reported for inciting racial hatred. And now here is Turkey sending us life-saving equipment. Politics is a filthy business. I've not seen any reference to this irony in the UK press yet.

This morning, we have news of the first Sikh doctor to die. He was an A&E specialist and died from Coronavirus picked up from his patients. A colleague describes him as being the 'father of the A&E team' at his hospital. There is a disproportionate number of Black, Asian and other ethnic minorities dying. I wonder if this sacrifice – these are key workers keeping the country running – will finally change Britain's view of itself. Will the British be more comfortable with its multi-ethnic identity? I have my doubts.

Few people are driving, as our ghostly, empty streets attest. So it's no surprise that the oil price is in freefall, and today has gone negative at minus US$35, with producers paying to have their oil stored. Financial markets have fallen around the world at this news.

The US, it appears, will have the highest death toll globally when the dust settles on Covid-19, yet all across the American Midwest people, encouraged by Trump, are protesting the lockdown. They say it is further evidence of heavy-handed Government, and is offensive to freeborn Americans who do not wish to be locked up in their own country. It beggars belief.

We are facing a heartbreaking decision: life or money. And, as ever, money is going to win. Crippled economies will lead to hunger, death, insurrection and more death, so some percentage of people are going to have to die to get the world working again; that is the brutal truth.

Unless a miracle cure is found, the death toll is not going to stop any time soon. But there are some small glimmers of hope. Plasma from Covid-19 survivors is already being trialled in the US as a vaccine, and everywhere scientists are working 24/7 to get a vaccine out with some signs that this may arrive sooner than the predicted 18 months.

Dominic and Steph are no longer allowed out of the Brighton marina on the 37ft yacht they call home. They are debating whether to continue fixing Jupiter up, to take her south to the Mediterranean later this summer, or to buy a bigger boat from which to run a charter business. I tell them it is a nice problem to have, as the price of boats must be falling like crazy. Meanwhile, they are both studying hard for their Ocean Yacht Master certification.

Our swallows are like ecstasy made flesh, as they swoop and dart and chirrup away in the sun, doing laps of the garden and slaloming over the roof of the old house. They are a daily reminder that life will go on with or without us and that Nature has its own agenda that works in centuries and millennia.

Our second delivery of meat from the High Street butcher has arrived, lamb chops and pork chops, mince and two chickens, as well as fruit and veg, gooseberry jam and sweet chilli sauce. That should keep us going for a week or two! The usual disinfecting rigmarole ensues: spraying the packaging with an antiseptic mist, and then washing our hands after packing it away.

Jan has suggested a walk to Pooh Bridge as it's another fine day. I count my blessings. While we can work, and our savings last, we can keep going like this for the foreseeable future.

We drive down to the parking area at the top of the long hill that runs down to Pooh Sticks Bridge and find it locked down, with a sign saying 'No Parking'. There must have been too many people doing this walk, so the forest rangers have closed it off. We turn around and head uphill and park just below the Enchanted Place and Gills Lap.

Jan is hit by a sudden headache, so we turn for home instead, and I return to the garden with Gus. Thinking about this hiccup, I realize just how fragile our security is. It may all appear chilled, sunny and peaceful, but I can see how easily disaster could strike. If one of us were to get really ill or have bad toothache, we would be running a gauntlet that could cost us both our lives. At one level, that statement and this feeling seems ridiculous, but I know that in reality it is all too true. You don't want to be going anywhere near a hospital or any kind of medical facility at present if it can be avoided. It is a sobering thought.

I go back in to check on Jan and find her lying on the sofa in the bedroom with the cat Saffy, her companion day and night, beside her. She says she feels much better, and later emerges with a blanket and cushions to lie on the lawn in the shade of the rowan tree, cat and dog on either side.

The old oak tree that stands just inside our western

neighbour's garden is today in full fig, its every leaf unfurled, the tree at its best and ready to sail through this summer majestically, as in every one of its previous 300 summers, little bothered by man's doings, a green battleship commanding our hill, sufficient unto itself. It is this tree's bare branches that provide the orchestral night music to my winter sleep as they thrash the wind that keens through their woody spaces, a kaleidoscope of greys and blacks highlighted by its night sailing partner the moon. But this afternoon, the oak is hove to, its green sails barely moving. It is our fifth week of lockdown.

CHAPTER 16

22nd April 2020

Nature continues to continue

Tonight, BBC Radio 3 will broadcast a 'Nightingale Concert' from a Hornbeam wood near Lewes in East Sussex, ten miles south of us, where seven nightingales have been making the night loud with their song this strange spring.

The birds will be joined by classical musicians in the broadcast, and by nature writer, Robert Macfarlane, with other writers and poets. They will be part of the human sounds joining the seven nightingales that tune up at 10pm each evening, singing from a blackthorn bush in the wood, joining hope and beauty and music in the cycle of life in this dark, sunlit spring.

I wonder, where is Tim Dee when he is needed? I am so enjoying the prose poem that is his wonderful book of spring and bird migration, titled 'Greenery'. I send news of the Nightingale Concert to my sister Jay and brother-in-law Guy in Cape Town and to naturalist Tim Dee, who is without doubt one of the UK's most eminent nature writers.

I know Jay and Guy, keen bird watchers, would give their eye teeth to hear this concert, and I send them links to it. They are connected to Tim through his wife, the ornithologist, Claire Spottiswoode, a close friend of their late son, Kirsten Louw, an ornithologist-botanist who died tragically young at 26, while studying for his doctorate at the University of Cape Town. But his name lives on through all those whose lives he touched, Claire among them, and also in the name of a rare Cape flower that he identified, 'Ornithogalum Kirstenii' and brought to the attention of the world of botany. It now bears his name. So in a way, the nightingales will be singing, unbeknown to them or their audience, a requiem for Kirsten, my lost nephew, thanks to the small South African audience I have alerted to the concert from the Hornbeam wood: Jay, Guy, Tim and Claire.

This morning, the Covid-19 news is led by word of the RAF flight that has finally brought in half the PPE kit from Turkey which is so desperately needed by nurses and doctors here in the UK. Thank you, Turkey!

The news also spotlights the fact that the UK opted out of a European Union joint purchasing drive to get PPE, for Brexit-led political reasons. The Government are falling over themselves to deny this and say the spokesperson on this issue 'misspoke', that treacherous slime of an excuse embodied in a word whose darkness underlines misdeeds wherever it is used.

It is becoming clear that death rates are statistically confusing. The average age of populations, its geographic density, its size, and the presence of international business and international airports, are all relevant when looking at deaths per 100,000. So the US and Britain slide down from the top slots to seventh and twelfth places, it would seem. The statisticians will doubtless be arguing over this for decades.

Meanwhile, anti-China propaganda is ramping up on social media at a rate of knots. Last night I received a conspiracy theory video asking why the virus did not go viral in China. Despite the fact that the country's two major cities, Beijing and Shanghai, are not far from Wuhan province where it originated, neither city was affected, says the video, even as the virus has run rampant in every country on earth. The video suggested that Covid-19 is a laboratory-manufactured tool, designed to undermine every economy on earth in order to give China increased global dominance. It was debunked almost as soon as it appeared. The fact that the Chinese provided the genetic structure of the virus as soon as they had it decoded is not mentioned.

The Covid-19 virus has unleashed another virus, this time man-made: the rumour mill that is working at capacity, full tilt, night and day. Conspiracy theories abound, and there is a glut of charlatans on the market, going so cheap we can all afford one of our own choice. They are a dime a dozen, which is not to say they are not dangerous. The world just now can ill afford them. And the Internet, so wonderful in so many ways, provides an instant global platform for the ranter as well as the most sophisticated academic with impeccable credentials, whose views skewed by politics are as dangerous as they seem credible.

On the home front, it is becoming clear that I am going to be in lockdown for at least another month or two, so I arrange to pay Georgie to look after my horse Callum for another month, and buy in another load of wood shavings for his bed. I miss riding a lot, especially in this glorious weather.

Last night, once again, we turned to our favourite TV series, *Ray Donovan*, which is life-enhancing in two respects: it takes our mind off the world's troubles, and in comparison to the challenges Ray Donovan faces in each episode, our life looks quite peachy.

Life goes on. Or not. The NHS is concerned that numbers attending hospital for non Covid-19 related illness, cancer or heart or liver issues, has fallen by 70 per cent. People will die at home for fear of seeking help at hospital.

Parliament has reopened today with a thin spread of MPs on the green leather benches in the house while others attend via the Internet. It is Wednesday, so it is Prime Minister's Question Time, the first led by Sir Keir Starmer, QC, human rights lawyer, and the new Labour leader. He asks his questions in a grave, forensic way about why the Government has been behind on every issue facing it with Covid-19; on testing, PPE, timing of the lockdown, and deaths in care homes. Dominic Raab, the Foreign Minister standing in for Boris, deals with the cross questioning as best he can, which, let's face it, is not all that well.

CHAPTER 17

23rd April 2020

The Emperor has no clothes

This Government is 'incompetent, inexperienced, floundering and an embarrassment' according to an off-the-record quote from just one of Boris's Tory supporters, who are horrified at the slow train crash they are watching unfold, as UK citizens die in their thousands, with no end in sight, and little evidence of a coherent plan. It is just what one might have expected from a Boris Johnson Government. Truly, the Emperor has no clothes.

The *New Scientist* reports: "The pandemic has already caused at least 41,000 deaths in the UK, according to a *Financial Times* analysis of 'excess deaths' data from the country's Office for National Statistics."

Amid this charnel-house news, there is evidence that some organisations are doing very well, thank you; proof that every cloud does indeed have a silver lining. Netflix gained nearly 16 million new subscribers in the first quarter of 2020, twice as many as predicted by analysts, as people turn to streaming to provide entertainment amid Coronavirus travel restrictions.

But not everyone is watching TV. Domestic violence rates are rising fast across the UK and Europe. *The Guardian* reports that domestic abuse killings have 'more than doubled' amid the Covid-19 lockdown. At least 16 suspected domestic abuse killings in the UK have been identified by campaigners since the Covid-19 lockdown restrictions were imposed, far higher than the average rate for the time of year, it has emerged.

Jan sends me information about Karen Ingala Smith, the founder of Counting Dead Women, a pioneering project that records the murders of women by men in the UK, who has identified at least 16 killings between March 23 and April 12, including those of children.

Ingala Smith's data records an average of five deaths for the same period over the past 10 years. Her findings for 2020, which are collated from Internet searches and people contacting her over social media, were raised during evidence to the Government Home Affairs select committee on Wednesday.

Dame Vera Baird QC, the Victims Commissioner for England and Wales, told MPs at the remote session: "Counting Dead Women has got to a total of 16 domestic abuse killings in the last three weeks. We usually say there are two a week, that looks to me like five a week, that's the size of this crisis."

It is unimaginable what some families, women in particular, have had to contend with during this time. While so many of us in lockdown have welcomed the additional peace and quiet to be creative, others have had to contend with a living hell. My heart goes out to them with the wish that when this time of suffering is over a happier future awaits them.

A newsflash: politicians have warned that the Government is considering a 'blanket ban' to prevent older people leaving their homes during the Coronavirus crisis. The health minister, Lord James Bethell, twice refused to deny that older people will be told to stay in extended lockdown in response to questions in the Lords on Wednesday.

"I was very concerned by the Government's refusal to answer my question," said Lord Blunkett, the former home secretary. "Older people must not be subjected to arbitrary incarceration as well as isolation."

Blunkett added: "The more the Government make restrictions age-related, rather than risk-related, the more they risk people pushing back very heavily and refusing to keep to the rules."

I smile at this exchange, imagining an army of the elderly, like me, frolicking in Britain's parks and on beaches to a Woodstock soundtrack, the hippy Sixties reclaimed just before death takes us on the final trip. To the American psychologist known for his strong advocacy of psychedelic drugs, Timothy Leary, I say: "Eat your heart out!"

Leary said: "My advice to people today is as follows: if you take the game of life seriously, if you take your nervous system seriously, if you take your sense organs seriously, if you take the energy process seriously, you must turn on, tune in, and drop out."

Well, Tim, old cock, we are sure as hell dropping out!

Another delight on today's news is that "Government scientists are expected to recommend against the public wearing medical face masks." WHO spokespeople are also saying that there is "little evidence that wearing masks stops the spread of Coronavirus." But people will still want masks, and there is plenty of evidence that they protect other people, should you be infected.

Meanwhile, in New York, two cats are the first confirmed cases of Coronavirus in companion animals in the US, federal officials reported yesterday, April 22. The cats, which had mild respiratory illnesses and are expected to recover, are thought to have contracted the virus from people in their households or neighbourhood. The finding, which comes after positive tests in some tigers and lions at the Bronx Zoo, adds to a small number of confirmed cases of the virus in animals worldwide.

The world is on track for an 'unprecedented' post-war recession, say countless news outlets, quoting an army of experts. Ratings agency Fitch says the world is heading for a recession of "unprecedented depth in the post-war period", with global gross domestic product predicted to tumble by 3.9 per cent in 2020. "This is twice as large as the decline anticipated in our early April GEO [global economic outlook] update and would be twice as severe as the 2009 recession," says Fitch's chief economist.

Turning away from the horror of this scenario, I read that the UK is planning to embark on a large-scale study of 300,000 people to find out what proportion of the population has already had the Coronavirus and how many may have some immunity to it as a result.

Studies are being undertaken around the world to work out how widespread the infection is. So far, they have found the proportion of people with antibodies showing they have been infected is low. The World Health Organisation said this week it appears that only around 2-3 per cent of people in the general population have been infected, with or without symptoms. So much for herd immunity.

The results of the British study will be crucial for planning a strategic endgame to the pandemic in the UK. Some 25,000 people will be invited to take part in the first wave of the study in England. It is expected it will be extended to 300,000 people over the next 12 months.

One of Britain's glories, our universities, are facing their own meltdown. Our academics are looking disaster in the face, as a report predicts a £2.5bn tuition fee loss for universities next year alongside the loss of 30,000 university jobs, based on gloomy predictions that both British and overseas students will stay away if the pandemic remains unchecked.

The Government is negotiating with the university sector to limit the number of students each institution can admit in September, in the hope that it will help some avoid cut-throat competition and possible bankruptcy if their student intake slumps. Supply and demand, that old killer, is alive and well alongside the pandemic.

Having a break from this news misery, I am greatly cheered by reading a recent essay by Philip Pullman, the novelist knighted in May for his services to literature, and perhaps best known for *His Dark Materials*, the fantasy trilogy about the adventures of the young heroine, Lyra Belacqua.

Pullman writes in a book of essays published by Penguin (and I agree with every word): "It's all got to change. If we come out of this crisis with all the rickety, fly-blown, worm-eaten old structures still intact, the same vain and indolent public schoolboys in charge, the same hedge fund managers stuffing their overloaded pockets with greasy fingers, our descendants will not forgive us. Nor should they. We must burn out the old corruption and establish a better way of living together.

"It's fitting that the Houses of Parliament are already falling down. We should begin there and tear the place down entirely, to rebuild it on a better plan. All the absurd ceremony, all the pegs for hanging up your sword, all the fake drama created by deliberately not having enough seats for every member and crowding through lobbies to vote, all the contemptible pomposity that only serves to tickle the fancy of those addicted to history-porn, the blazing stupidity of maintaining seats for hereditary peers – away with it.

'And let's reform the voting system. At the very least, let's do that without delay. It's no wonder that people feel disconnected from politics when most of us live in safe seats, and might as well not vote at all. We must be able to see that our opinions are accurately reflected in the composition of our Government, not completely disregarded as they are now. So it might lead to coalitions: excellent. Discussion, compromise, working together, are exactly how to run a decent country.

"Then we must educate our children properly. It is quite extraordinary that one school, Eton College, should have such a hold on the high places of politics. It's also extraordinary, and scandalous, that the magnificent facilities and opportunities that the public schools (the commercial schools, as A.H. Halsey liked to call them) offer to their pupils are not equally available to every child. The present dreary culture of mechanistic tests and meaningless league tables and invented fetishes like 'fronted adverbials' should be swept away like filthy cobwebs; children need light and drama and music and poetry and science and art and curiosity and libraries and plenty of grass to play on, and plenty of time to run about and fool around.

'We should start by abolishing the tax privileges the commercial schools benefit from by pretending to be charities, and pour money into the schools most children go to.

"If it turns out to be true that the Government for Brexit-related reasons refused to take part in the procurement advantage offered by EU Governments, thus making it harder for the NHS to deal with the Covid-19 and placing thousands of people at risk, the entire front bench ought to resign. But of course they won't: they have not a single grain of shame. So they should be arraigned on charges of conspiracy to murder. Nothing less will do. They knew the risks, and thought they'd rather appease the foaming zealots of Brexit.

"And now the circumstances have changed so profoundly, we must hold back on Brexit itself. There are so many clear advantages to being in the EU, and the benefits of leaving are so tenuous and fanciful, that we must revisit the referendum and hope that this time the Labour Party under a new leader will play a proper part in the argument; and that the lies, the cheating, the flagrant and shameless mendacity will be fully exposed by a strong, passionate, and focused campaign to remain.

"There's so much more that needs to be done, but this is how I think we should start. The way we allow ourselves to be governed at the moment looks like the triumph of habit over putrefaction. We can't go on like this."

Phillip Pullman, I say: "Amen to that." When I hear a voice like his, I wonder why we are unable to attract people of his calibre to government? If we get the governments we deserve, then we are all culpable in this mess. And that is a truly sobering thought.

CHAPTER 18
24th April 2020

Intersecting triangles of support

Lying in bed this morning, listening to the birdsong and enjoying my first coffee of the day, my thoughts go out to those people with whom I am most closely walking this walk and how much they mean to me. There is, as they say, nothing like a hanging to concentrate the mind. I've just listened to a podcast of a 60-year-old Bristol-based-pilot who survived the virus in intensive care, and it has made me think some sobering thoughts.

Inevitably, it's made me think about death and about my own possible demise, and they take me out of my sunlit bedroom across the world to family and friends whose daily emails and calls are helping me to cope with our current troubling reality.

There are intersecting triangles that start with my wife, Jan, here at home with me, our son Dominic and his partner Stephanie in Brighton Marina and our daughter Imogen, staying near Rye with her godmother. Then, further afield, there is a three-cornered construct that forms the other part of my intimate world, the tight links 6,000 miles south to my sister Jay and brother-in-law Guy in Cape Town, South Africa, and 6,000 miles due west across the Atlantic and the US to my brother Herman and my sister-in-law Teri, in Santa Barbara, California.

Then there is my sister's daughter, Nikki Louw in Cape Town, and Jan's sister Gail and her husband Tich in Bristol, from whom I hear regularly too.

I am lucky also to hear regularly from friends, Ivan in Exeter, Devon, Elma in Johannesburg, Jacques and Barbara in Cape Town, Richard in Cape Town, Larry in Melbourne, and Adrienne just down the road from us, near Eastbourne.

Each of these people have enriched my life greatly with their love and friendship and have helped me survive mentally, physically, financially and in so many other ways too, with laughter and good advice and the odd admonition too, when I've needed it, but which was perhaps not always appreciated at the time.

These people make up my tribe, my landscape, my world to a greater degree than they might imagine. If I die, it is in their hearts and minds that my life will echo longest.

Before I can get any more maudlin, I am cheered to hear on BBC Radio 4 that a week from today, human trials on a vaccine will begin here in the UK. Volunteers are being interviewed on the radio. There will be two groups,: the first will get the Covid-19 vaccine, the second will get a jab against meningitis as a control. They have been told not to put themselves in danger, and to abide by Government regulations on social distancing. Scientists at Bristol, Oxford and other universities are working flat out on research they have been doing on the Coronavirus for some years, and they sound hopeful.

The debate about how long we will be in lockdown has got a little clearer this Friday morning, April 25. It seems it will not be totally lifted until June. The great fear is that if we get a second or even a third wave, these could be worse than the first, matching what happened with the 1918 Spanish Flu epidemic that killed 50 million people worldwide.

During the day, I issue another story for H&H Classics, on a 1970 Dodge Challenger like the one in the 1997 cult movie *Vanishing Point* with its car chase across America. It is estimated to sell for £60,000 to £80,000. The story generates a fair amount of press interest. Among the responses is a note from Jim Waterson, the Media correspondent of the Guardian, who sends the following note: "Julian, I have no idea why you put me on your mailing list and the chances of me covering any of your quirky auction items are zero, but I absolutely adore the weird details of your emails and they are a constant delight. Thank you in these strange times, Jim."

I Google him and find that he is a Jesus College Oxford history graduate. I write back to apologise for sending him press releases he is not interested in and say I will remove his name from my mailing lists. I add my thanks for his amusing note, which as a *Guardian* reader myself, and husband of a former *Guardian* journalist, I very much appreciate. He replies immediately, as follows: "No please do not remove me! I adore them. The Cheshire wood piece a few months ago gave me enormous delight. I just wanted to respond." I thank him and say I will continue to include him in mailings.

I share this exchange with my client, Damian Jones, Head of Sales with H&H Classics who reveals that his brother Sam Jones is *The Guardian's* correspondent in Madrid, whose copy about Covid-19 in Spain I have been reading for weeks. It is such a small world, as we are currently being reminded. Sam then reaches out by email himself to say hello, and to say too what a small world it was. We are all connected.

In the evening, Jan and I take Gus for a walk on the Forest, the big central section that we call the 'Big Bowl' which runs down to a little waterfall in the stream known as the 'Garden of Eden'. There are very few people about at 6pm, just three sets of dog walkers and two lads on mountain bikes we pass on our hour-long stroll. The temperature, after a warm sunny day, is still around 20 degrees, and the petrol and coconut smell off the huge waves of bright yellow flowers on the gorse bushes is all around us. We stroll with Gus up to the high point stand of pines, and sit on a bench there looking west towards the lowering sun. It's peaceful, and no-one could guess that the world was in turmoil.

It's strange what you focus on in this time and food

plays a large part. You can be forgiven for wondering if, as Rupert Brooke asked: "Is there honey still for tea?" With death stalking us, it seems a trivial concern.

I'm sitting in the garden today, working on a client request to analyse the art and wine markets for the past 40 years, from 1980 to 2020, from an investment perspective. My time at Bonhams still gives me insights as well as access to art market specialists and Masters of Wine. I reach out to everyone who may be able to help and start typing fast.

But it feels good to have a deadline and have my feet held to the fire once more. Life goes on, and this job is a wonderful way to escape all worries about the virus for a few hours.

There have been huge changes in art market investment potential over the past 30 years. At the end of the 1980s, we had the Impressionist boom, fuelled by Japan, which burst almost overnight as the decade turned, and the Japanese economy tanked. Since then, the general growth in the art market, combined with its globalisation, particularly with the development of the internet, has created a much more stable series of micro markets that are not so dependent on just a few investors.

While trophy works by blue chip names in the Contemporary and Modern Art markets – Jean-Michel Basquiat, Andy Warhol, Jeff Koons, Francis Bacon – remain the most bankable of any artworks as they sell for tens or even hundreds of millions of dollars, they depend on a relatively small selection of ultra-high net worth collectors, which renders that area of the market potentially volatile.

Key to the rise of the art market as an alternative investment market was the financial crash at the end of 2008. With even bonds and gilts affected like never before, the relative risk of investing in art diminished and a whole industry grew up around that, including everything from specialist investment funds to new investment arms of existing banks.

From 2003 to 2015, the most successful investment market of all – not just within the global art market – was the classic car market, and although that has softened, micro markets within it, for cars from the 70s and 80s, have picked up. Modern British Art has also enjoyed a second wave of success in the past ten years or so, as collectors have moved beyond the Abstract Expressionists to invest in the previously lesser celebrated representational artists, such as Eric Ravilious, Edward Bawden and the artists of Great Bardfield, as well as other names who have come into the limelight and been selling for tens if not hundreds of thousands of pounds, like Cedric Morris.

Looking to the future, areas to watch include Contemporary African Art and Photography, African-American Fine Art, Post-War design, especially Scandinavian Furniture, studio pottery and designer jewellery from the late 1960s onwards, like Grima and Kutchinsky. Other areas that do consistently well are designer watches and rare limited-edition toys in their original boxes or packaging, especially Star Wars figures. If you're going to buy any of this, buy the best you can afford as that is what will accrue more value in the long term.

On the subject of investing in wine, the situation is simpler. I am briefed by Richard Harvey, a Master of Wine and head of Bonhams Wine & Whisky Department. Most fine wines, particularly Bordeaux, outperformed most other investments from the mid-1980's through to around 2011. Since then, it has really been only top Burgundy that has increased in value significantly, but even that has fallen back in the past year. Richard says: "Apart from these two areas, vintage Champagne, some top Italian, Californian and Australian wines have performed well."

When thinking of investing in the art market, the financial and stock markets have much to teach us. The first principle is to educate yourself, or use experts whose advice you trust, because they have delivered for friends and people you know over a long time.

The art market goes in seven-year cycles, so in the 40 years we are talking about, there have been five separate periods of highs and lows. Art and wine are both subject to fashion, just because an artist is doing well in one period does not mean he or she will always be doing well. Just like a company on the stock market.

Currently, for reasons of the world economy and Brexit coming on top of a general slowdown, the art market is depressed. In fact, it is no coincidence that the art market follows the curve of the international financial markets – when rich people are flush with money, they spend more on luxuries, and art is the ultimate luxury.

When buying or selling, the art and wine auction markets are very useful as they are to some extent transparent – you know what something sold for, so there is a benchmark. Private art gallery sales and private wine dealers do not offer prices achieved to the public. Study auction market results: they are a rapid way to learn about what is hot and what is not.

Sage advice to would-be investors in the art or wine markets is to follow your heart and your taste buds, because then, if your purchase falls in value, you will still own something you enjoy.

As I finish writing, I wonder to myself why anyone just now is even thinking of alternative investment opportunities. But of course, it is people who think like this who will bounce back fastest, make a quick buck soonest, and be off and running in the rat race the moment the starter pistol goes off. Such is the way of the world, and the Coronavirus is not going to change that.

CHAPTER 19

25th April 2020

Playing chicken with Covid-19

The two miniature apple trees on the lawn are now in full bloom, and a mass of white and faint pink blossom stands out against the green of the grass, with the maroon of the Japanese Acer in wonderful contrast, a subject for Impressionism if ever I saw one. I planted these two small trees about four years ago, and now each autumn they produce a freight of small round red apples on one and larger red and green apples on the other. The grass is needing a trim again, I notice.

Jan has been kind enough to wrestle with my car insurers this morning to get our breakdown service out to fix my car's dead battery. Living out here in the sticks at a time like this, we want to have both cars in good working order. But no joy, I am not covered for home visits to fix dead batteries. Next she rings her bank, which promptly sends an AA man out as she is insured to drive my car.

The news this morning is led by an NHS plea to heart, stroke and cancer patients to seek help if they are having issues or need a regular check-up. The spokesman says the NHS has not been overwhelmed, as had been feared, and is there for everyone as usual. He says hospitals are coping. I heard yesterday that our local hospital at Pembury is now divided into two sections, one for Covid and one for everything else, with two separate entrances. I also hear that a broadcaster who went into hospital has died of Covid-19; it's not clear if he picked it up there or went in with it. It is clear, however, that people are terrified of going anywhere near a hospital at present.

My younger brother, Herman, has always been braver than the average man. Now he is taking on a new and very dangerous opponent, the virus itself, on behalf of his employer, a textile firm in LA. He has driven the 400 miles north from his home in Santa Barbara to San Francisco to seal a deal for personal protective clothing, which he reckons could become a huge opportunity for his employer and in the process get PPE to the medical frontline instead of sitting in Chinese warehouses, hopefully saving lives in the process. He says what was going to be a quick two-day dash to San Francisco has turned into four days of trying to close the deal.

I tell him he is not being wise for putting his own life at risk, playing Chicken with Covid-19. It is one of the advantages of my being the eldest sibling, and him the youngest; I feel free to tell him of my concerns. But he says he is being careful, staying in a hotel that has a skeleton staff: he does not see the irony. The hotel, he adds, does not feed you, or sanitise your room until you leave. Sounds dodgy as hell to me, but once Herman has the bit between his teeth, there is no stopping him.

In the midst of Hurricane Sandy in October 2012, he drove hundreds of miles to get *into* New York for a business meeting when it was being flooded. Everyone else except for the rescue services, were staying indoors or fleeing the city as the storm wreaked havoc.

Hurricane Sandy was the deadliest and most destructive hurricane of the 2012 Atlantic hurricane season, inflicting nearly $70 billion in damage. Its storm surge hit New York City and flooded streets, tunnels and subway lines, cutting off the city's power. Herman powered through it all, and I love him for it, but he is too brave by half at times. It was F.

Scott Fitzgerald who said: 'Action is Character' and in Herman's case, his character often demands action that I and others would see as risky. But there is no arguing with him.

This is the reason I never flew with him in any aircraft he piloted in his youth. I did not trust him to bring me back in one piece. Years later, when he was no longer flying, he admitted to the odd occasion when he'd landed the small plane with just petrol fumes left in the tank. That said, he is a good chap to have in your corner when your back is to the wall and the chips are down. He has cojones to spare. I wish I had some more of that quality myself.

Yesterday I tried to resuscitate my Panasonic bread maker, unused for 18 years, but no joy. I'm not sure if it was the machine or my inability to programme it that was at fault. I had to scrape out all the ingredients I put in its mixer to make a wholemeal loaf and instead do an old-fashioned reliable hand knead and bake in the oven as usual. Surprisingly, it turned out very well: in fact I would say that it's the best loaf I've made yet.

I have a long chatty email from my sister Jay in Cape Town. She and Guy seem to have things very much under control. She writes: "We seem to be managing reasonably well so far during the lockdown. In fact we have been very strict about going anywhere, apart from Guy taking the cars for a quick run to keep the batteries going. Nikki has very kindly been doing a weekly shop for us and we have been using various online delivery services. We had intended to walk around the garden briskly for half an hour each day, but that very quickly fell by the wayside! Our exercise now consists of some exercises for the elderly which are supposed to help with balance! Walking up and down the stairs is also part of it, and my fitness levels being abysmal, I am short of breath by the end.

"Guy has his workspace in the studio upstairs. He beavers away diligently for eight hours a day, often more than that. There have been video conference calls and many sketches of pipes and fittings and other engineering mysteries rapidly executed. I am amazed at how often he wakes up in the morning having solved a design problem. On the weekends and public holidays, he goes at it like a battery bunny – seeing to the pool, painting and scraping, cutting back the garden and on and on. Sometimes the ceaseless toil makes me feel guilty, but I'm trying not to compare.

"My contribution is mainly housework and cooking with a bit of gardening thrown in too. I baked my first loaf of bread this morning and it turned out surprisingly well! Anna is much missed. Her once a week stint cleaning for us has always given me more time to do my things and I appreciate her contribution greatly. She is on paid leave until it is safe for her, and us, to return. Her parents and two children are in Zimbabwe, and she misses them very much during this difficult time. I have taken time to bead every day, and you are much in my thoughts as I sew away. It is such a pleasure and release for me and truly takes me to a different space. The news becomes addictive. I try not to watch too much, as the figures and suffering are so great and some of the politicians utterly infuriating. Donald Trump is a monster and a frighteningly stupid one at that – what is wrong with the Americans?!"

My sister speaks for millions.

Dom and Steph on their boat in Brighton Marina say they are working hard on their navigation course. We have a good catch-up and talk boats at length. Currently, they like the look of an aluminium expedition boat designed by Ed Joy and built in Cape Town. How strange it would be if they bought a South African boat!

I walk down the back hill to see Callum, who is near the gate of his paddock for once, swathed in his summer anti-fly rug and mask. I speak to him quietly about this strange time and say I hope he is enjoying his holiday. We will in time return to our old haunts on the Forest, I promise him, and promise too that we will take our time getting fit together again. He does not say much, but my impression is that he is easy with things as they are and in no rush to have me on his back once more, traipsing miles over Ashdown Forest. For him, life is pretty good. I give him the carrot he knows is concealed in my back pocket, and after a head rub, I leave him to his grass and go in search of lunch myself.

CHAPTER 20

26th April 2020

The stroke paralysing America

It is Sunday, but it feels just like every other day of the week. There is birdsong and silence, and a sense that we have all the time in the world, when in fact, in my case, I know that is far from true. The handful of tablets I take each night to regulate my heart and my blood tell me that clearly, and now there is a pandemic devastating life for people in Britain and around the world. I may not have as much time as I think I have.

The papers announce that the official UK hospital death count reached 20,000 today.

I go down to make coffee and let the cat out of the kitchen. Saffy yowls, annoyed at not being upstairs last night. But she is now 14 years old and her bladder, like mine, is shot. Like me she can't last a night without a pee and so disturbs Jan who has never been the best sleeper, so she is relegated to her basket in the kitchen, allowed up once more in the morning.

After making the coffee, I go out into the front garden to greet the day, and a beautiful day it is too. I remember John Humphries, the acerbic host of the BBC Radio 4 *Today* programme, moaning endlessly over the years about too much sunshine and saying it was time for some decent rain; his garden needed it. I suppose he might describe the weather as 'relentlessly beautiful'. It is such strange weather for a time of plague; rain and gales and dark lowering skies like those in 18th century oil paintings would somehow seem more appropriate. But we have had sunshine for week after week in the most spectacular spring I can remember.

Standing in the garden, I see that the wisteria has sent out runners and reached the storm porch, its soft blue flowers unfurling against a yellow-leaved bush whose name I don't know. The scent of the lilac bushes in the side hedge by the wicket gate is heady; they now stand ten feet tall, and are heavy with bunches of bloom in pale and dark lilac.

On the way back from checking on Callum yesterday, I ran into Ethan, the seven-year-old son of our neighbours Terry and Michelle. He is in the big chicken coop at the top of their garden where it abuts ours. He calls out: "Hello Julian!" something I find so touching every time he does it. He is such a confident little boy; his parents are doing well by him. I ask him how his two orphan lambs are doing and he says: "They're back with their friends in the field now. They can eat grass." I ask how the chickens are performing on the egg-laying front and he says: "We get one big one and two small ones every morning." I congratulate him on this happy harvest, and climb over our fence behind the stables.

Another neighbour from around the corner, Miles, delivers coffee, salted almonds, and carrots which his wife Belinda kindly bought for us at Waitrose. In return, we give him a vacuum pack of dried yeast from our restaurant suppliers that Belinda has been unable to source. We offer each other our parcels gingerly, with fingertip transfers. And the talk is of Dominic and yachting. Miles has sailed a bit himself, he says, and is interested in hearing about the yachting vlogs that rekindled Dom's life on the water after his teenage love of sailing. I promise to email him links to some of my favourites.

Adrienne, my friend and work colleague these past ten years, sends me a document to proof. It is a pitch she has written for the South African Chamber of Commerce for a fundraising campaign on behalf of South Africa's President Cyril Ramaphosa's Solidarity Fund. The President is reaching out to the South African diaspora in the hope of attracting money to support the country through the pandemic crisis, and I will do the media element if we get the job. The country was in deep financial trouble even before the virus hit. The former President, Jacob Zuma, used his time in office to steal billions with the help of the corrupt Indian family the Guptas, who are now in hiding in Dubai. The country is in dire straits.

But it's not only South Africa that occupies my thoughts.

The Atlantic magazine has a brilliant feature article by staff writer George Packer about America, headlined: *We Are Living in a Failed State: The Coronavirus Didn't Break America. It Revealed What Was Already Broken.*

He writes: "When the virus came here, it found a country with serious underlying conditions, and it exploited them ruthlessly. Chronic ills – a corrupt political class, a sclerotic bureaucracy, a heartless economy, and a divided and distracted public – had gone untreated for years. We had learned to live, uncomfortably, with the symptoms. It took the scale and intimacy of a pandemic to expose their severity – to shock Americans with the recognition that we are in the high-risk category."

He continues: "The crisis demanded a response that was swift, rational, and collective. The United States reacted instead like Pakistan or Belarus – like a country with shoddy infrastructure and a dysfunctional Government whose leaders were too corrupt or stupid to head off mass suffering. The administration squandered two irretrievable months to prepare. From the president came willful blindness, scapegoating, boasts, and lies. From his mouthpieces, conspiracy theories and miracle cures. A few senators and corporate executives acted quickly – not to prevent the coming disaster, but to profit from it. When a Government doctor tried to warn the public of the danger, the White House took the mic and politicized the message."

Packer concludes: "Every morning in the endless month of March, Americans woke up to find themselves citizens of a failed state. With no national plan – no coherent instructions at all – families, schools, and offices were left to decide on their own whether to shut down and take shelter. When test kits, masks, gowns, and ventilators were found to be in desperately short supply, governors pleaded for them from the White House, which stalled, then called on private enterprise, which couldn't deliver. States and cities were forced into bidding wars that left them prey to price gouging and corporate profiteering. Civilians took out their sewing machines to try to keep ill-equipped hospital workers healthy and their patients alive. Russia, Taiwan, and the United Nations sent humanitarian aid to the world's richest power – a beggar nation in utter chaos."

The article goes on to unpack the disaster in the US with forensic skill and devastating insights.

Another good read reaches me from *The Guardian*. The brilliant author, Yuval Noah Harari asks: 'Will Coronavirus change our attitudes to death? Quite the opposite.'

The modern world, he says, 'has been shaped by the belief that humans can outsmart and defeat death. That was a revolutionary new attitude. For most of history, humans meekly submitted to death. Up to the late modern age, most religions and ideologies saw death not only as our inevitable fate, but as the main source of the meaning in life. The most important events of human existence happened after you exhaled your last breath. Only then did you come to learn the true secrets of life. "Only then did you gain eternal salvation, or suffer everlasting damnation. For most of history, the best human minds were busy giving meaning to death, not trying to defeat it.

"As humans, we have been so successful in our attempt to safeguard and prolong life that our worldview has changed in a profound way. While traditional religions considered the afterlife as the main source of meaning, from the 18th century ideologies such as liberalism, socialism and feminism lost all interest in the afterlife."

And he concludes:

"When the present crisis is over, I don't expect we will see a significant increase in the budgets of philosophy departments. But I bet we will see a massive increase in the budgets of medical schools and healthcare systems."

I must agree with Hariri, but wonder if the Coronavirus will not force the pendulum to swing back a little to a new interest in what happens after life. But that is a forlorn hope; there is no knowing what lies beyond. Death remains a profound mystery, however much we've been forced to confront it during this time of Covid-19.

As I write, I am enveloped in the scent of the yellow Peace rose at the top of our garden and my mind wanders to my late mother, Elise Louw. What would she have said about all this, the pandemic? What if anything has it taught us? And, as ever, she comes up with a humdinger:

"My kind, ons moet leer om in vreede saam te lewe of ons gaan almal alleen sterwe." My child, we must learn to live together in peace, or we are all going to die alone."

I breathe deep of the Peace rose scent, and then I breathe some more.

CHAPTER 21

27th April 2020

The health or wealth tug-of-war

Health or wealth? This is now the question – life for all of us, or economic death for Britain. This is the burning question, now that the hospitals have proved themselves able to cope with the worst of the pandemic and the curve of new infections has flattened. With light at the end of the tunnel, albeit a dim one, the country's business community is bestirring itself.

I wake up early this Monday, uneasy, and for the first time anxious, because I can hear the tug-of-war on this issue of health versus wealth. The voices of commerce and finance are beginning to speak up louder about reopening the country for work, business and pleasure. What is the point of lockdown and furlough, they ask, if when people go back to their jobs, they find no companies to work for?

But if lockdown is lifted, what are the chances of a second wave of infection, worse than the first? This is the conundrum facing Boris and his cabinet. Boris Johnson, our absentee Prime Minister, is returning to work today, April 27, after his three-week absence from the UK cockpit and his brush with death. On Friday, Boris had a three-hour catch up session with his cabinet.

First thing this morning, in good time for the lunchtime news, Boris appeared on the steps of Number 10 Downing Street to make a statement. There will be no let-up on lockdown yet, he said, speaking with something of his old energy and brio. "We are now beginning to turn the tide" on the disease. But, he added, he refused to "throw away" the public's "effort and sacrifice" and relax the lockdown too soon.

He apologised for being "away from my desk for much longer than I would've liked" and thanked his colleagues who stood in for him – as well as the public for their "sheer grit and guts".

He said he understood concerns from business-owners who were impatient to end the lockdown. But ending it too soon could lead to a second spike in cases and cause more deaths, 'economic disaster' and restrictions being reintroduced, he said. "I ask you to contain your impatience."

He said there were "real signs now that we are passing through the peak" – including fewer hospital admissions and fewer Covid-19 patients in intensive care.

And comparing the outbreak to someone being attacked, Boris said: "If this virus were a physical assailant, an unexpected and invisible mugger – which I can tell you from personal experience, it is – then this is the moment when we have begun together to wrestle it to the floor."

The sad truth is that had Boris got his act together earlier, even a week earlier, thousands would be alive today who are dead. And the life and death struggle of 'wrestling to the floor' this desperately dangerous enemy would not have required so much muscle. Boris has been as much of a problem to continued life in Britain, as the virus itself. In him, Covid-19 found a complacent opponent.

He goes on to say that the UK has "so far collectively shielded our NHS" and "flattened the peak" - but he could not yet say when or which restrictions would be lifted to ease lockdown.

Indeed, our citizenry have behaved impeccably on the whole, led by a Government that must face a tribunal at the end of this catastrophe, which has every indication of ending with Britain shown to have paid a most terrible and unnecessary price.

Meanwhile, Italy is starting a phased reopening, and New Zealand announces that it has halted the public spread of Covid-19 infection. Spain has let its children out on the streets, as long as they stay within a kilometre of home and are accompanied by an adult. Some form of 'normal' life is returning to Europe, slowly, painfully, with grandmother's footsteps.

London's underground system is running 95 per cent empty – the 5 per cent are NHS staff and essential workers, I suppose. The BBC interview a young woman travelling alone, who says she is off to the country to look after her mother, who is suffering from the painful condition known as fibromyalgia.

James Dart, a *Guardian* journalist and commentator, offers the following comment – words that pithily sum it all up for me.

"For four years, we allowed the hard Right to peddle the ludicrous myth that the UK was in some way superior, exceptional, unique. They told us it was the EU that was holding us back. They made unsubstantiated claim after unsubstantiated claim about power and control.

"They unleashed demons by using nationalistic, populist language, dividing communities and dragging politics further into the gutter. They mercilessly and shamefully went after all who dared to oppose them, and on occasion, they weaponised racism and bigotry to court the far Right.

"As we pass the 20,000-death mark, remember that it is these same people who failed to act on the findings of the 2016 Cygnus Report, or the more urgent 2019 warnings, or their January and February head start. They lamented Italy, but did nothing.

"Remember that it is these same people who spent those months peacocking in front of their base, talking up Big Ben bongs, skipping COBRA meetings, and holidaying abroad.

"Remember that it is these people who lied to the British people about their *political* decision not to work with the EU on procuring life-saving ventilators.

"Remember that it is these people who have utterly failed to show that the UK is in any way a leader in the modern world, allowing its people to die, failing to work with its allies and failing to stand up to the lunacy of Donald Trump. How can any nation claim to be a leader, or exceptional, or superior, whilst it lets its doctors and nurses go to work in bin bags?

"These are extremists; wolves in wolves' clothing, nonchalantly parading their cluelessness, their heartlessness, and their deluded sense of Old World entitlement to the world without a care in the world.

"If you're not seething, then I'm sorry to say it, but you're part of the problem." Well said James, I and thousands of others are with you on this!

In *The Financial Times*, the UK's Office of National Statistics offers dire figures: "…the true death toll from Covid-19 in the UK is now 41,000, which is 600 per million citizens, the highest death toll in the world." Well done, Boris, you and your mates have played a blinder.

A client has been in touch to ask if I would like to do more work in Africa. When this horror lifts, I look forward to flying south. I allow myself to dream a little and think of the parts of Africa I would like to revisit besides South Africa, and I am instantly transported to the sea-facing terrace of the Polana Hotel in Maputo, capital of Mozambique.

Some 50 years ago, I sat down to one of the greatest meals of my life in the restaurant on that terrace – huge local prawns caught offshore that day, grilled with butter and garlic, a glass of ice cold Vinho Verde and a small hot freshly baked loaf of bread. Sheer heaven. The memory of that meal, taken amid the floral smells of a tropical night and the scents worn by exotically-dressed women eating out with their white-suited men, lives on in my mind and I would love to revisit that part of Africa, so damaged by war since my memorable meal at the Polana.

And then serendipity strikes. It's a telephone call from the owner of a safari park some 300 miles south of the Polana Hotel. He wants help selling the place. He thinks it will be years before tourists return in sufficient numbers to make it a viable concern again. So now he wants to sell it as an environmentally unspoiled bolthole for a billionaire with interest in nature and Africa. I ask him to outline his offer and promise to get it to some property people I know in London with wealthy Chinese and Russian clients, one of whom has just paid £200m for Britain's most expensive house, a stone's throw from Buckingham Palace. The asking price for the safari park is a snip for what is undoubtedly something akin to the Garden of Eden.

My horse Callum's current carer, Georgie, texts me to say that Milord is now in his summer pasture in front of our cottage. So by looking out of the window I can keep an eye on him, and with my binoculars I can see the very whites of his eyes under his fly mask.

The birdbath in the garden, which I cleaned out yesterday and refilled, has been discovered by the avian community today and they are putting it to good use, the weather still sunny and warm.

I mow the lawn one more time, and afterwards sit on the steamer chair under the umbrella – my summer office – admiring the stripes on the grass. Gus lies in front of me, looking back at me lazily from time to time, counting the minutes to lunch and the chance of scraps. I look closely at him, as his neck seems to have disappeared and his head enters his shoulders directly. Maybe no scraps today!

The swallows are in a mating frenzy, the noise from them in the stables and over the garden is a high-pitched joy. They rocket in and out of the open top half of the stable doors like F18 jets launching and landing on an aircraft carrier. You'd think, after flying 6,000 miles long haul, with no beef, chicken or veggie options, they'd be bloody exhausted, but no, it's Viagra City here at the top of the garden. Reminds me a bit of Fourth Beach Clifton in Cape Town, half century ago, with the smell of coconut oil and pheromones rising from the oiled teenage torsos, the ice-cold Atlantic doing nothing to calm the sexual frisson one little bit.

Chapter 22

28th April 2020

The Royals in lockdown

It is a cool, wet day for the first time in six weeks. I'm glad that I cut the lawn yesterday, but annoyed that I did not put the garden furniture away last night as its soft cushions are all soaked. But reading the papers this morning, I feel ashamed about my worry over garden furniture getting wet.

Global virus cases passed the three million mark today, with more than 200,000 deaths, according to Johns Hopkins University in the US, which is tracking the spread of the pandemic.

Here in Britain, there will be a one-minute silence today at 11am for key workers who have died. I stand silent in the shower as the pips for 11am go off, thinking of the dead as the water beats hard on my head.

The Government announced last night that compensation payments of £60,000 will be made to families of key workers who've died from Covid-19. But, not unexpectedly, bereaved families say the money cannot make up for their loss. There will doubtless be a reckoning after this is all over. I do hope so.

The newspapers and TV show that London is a ghost

city, and the only people out at night are knife-wielding drug dealers and rough sleepers, some of whom worked in cafes and restaurants that closed six weeks ago. Many of the normal charity food and soup kitchens are not currently open, and people are starving on the streets of London.

There are restaurants that have turned themselves into impromptu charity soup kitchens, but they are few and far between.

Despite Boris saying yesterday that there would be no end to lockdown yet, for fear of losing all we've gained, thanks to the public's sacrifice of staying home, there are commercial voices today calling for their businesses to reopen – gyms, food markets, garden centres. The garden centre spokesman makes the best case, saying they have the space for social distancing, and gardening is the perfect activity for people stuck at home; he also mentions the mental health benefits of gardening. All good stuff. But for now, the Government is hanging tough.

The football world is looking into ways of starting to play again behind closed doors, and F1 motor racing is planning to race at all their venues with no public in the stands. So strange, so very surreal.

Thank God for gossip. It is the yeast that lifts our spirits. Lockdown has meant that one of Britain's national treasures, writer and playwright Alan Bennett, now gets a hot lunch. Bennett is known for – among other plays turned into films – *The Madness of King George* (1991) and *The History Boys* (2004).

In an interview this morning, he says that his civil partner, Rupert Thomas, editor of the design and decoration magazine, *The World of Interiors*, usually works away from home and likes a hot lunch. So now with both of them stuck at home, there is a hot lunch served for both of them. It is a charming insight into the living arrangements of this delightful man who has so enriched British life. I am glad you are getting a hot lunch, Mr Bennett!

I love his wit and wisdom. Some of his quotes about books stay with me as both have so enriched my life. Half my life has been reading, the other half writing. Or, as Bennett says: "You don't put your life into your books, you find it there."

"The best moments in reading," the boys' teacher Hector says in his *The History Boys,* which Jan took us all to as a Christmas treat years ago, "are when you come across something – a thought, a feeling, a way of looking at things – which you had thought special and particular to you. Now here it is, set down by someone else, a person you have never met, someone even who is long dead. And it is as if a hand has come out and taken yours."

The pandemic and *The Daily Express* newspaper have lifted the lid on the royal living arrangements of Her Majesty the Queen and Prince Philip, who have been in lockdown in Windsor Castle for six weeks. Normally, the couple live apart, the irascible Duke at Wood Farm on the royal estate at Sandringham in Norfolk, and the Queen in London, at Buckingham Palace.

The Express reports: "The Duke of Edinburgh attended royal events at his wife's side for decades, finally retiring from duty in 2017 at the impressive age of 96. Since then, Philip has enjoyed a break away from the Windsor bubble and is reported to split his time between Buckingham Palace and Wood Farm, Norfolk. While the Queen remains busy with royal duty in Windsor, Prince Philip enjoys a slower pace of life, painting and reading." Hopefully no longer terrorising other road users with his appalling driving. But I imagine that being stuck at Windsor may not be improving the royal temper.

Other couples are not as fortunate to have farms and palaces to give them space. *The Guardian* reports: *Calamitous: domestic violence is set to soar by 20 per cent during global lockdown.*

At least 15 million more cases of domestic violence are predicted this year as a result of pandemic restrictions, according to new data.

Thinking of domestic violence, I raise my eyes to King's Standing, a group of pines crowning the hill that dominates our southern skyline, named for Henry VIII's hunting visits to what was once one of his royal deer parks. At sunset, the trees are a black clump on the horizon. In my mind's eye, I see a young Henry VIII standing there, bow in hand, waiting for deer to be driven past him for a killing shot. Beside him is the beautiful young Anne Boleyn, whom he is courting. Her family home, the lovely, moated Hever Castle, is just five miles to the north. The poor girl has no idea of the horror awaiting her. She is about to marry the poster boy for domestic violence. This valley of ours has played a number of supporting roles in English history. Our present troubles fade into insignificance when compared to Tudor England with its religious changing of the guard and all the bloodshed to which that led.

Chefs and restaurant owners across Europe fear bankruptcy as the continent's gastronomic culture remains in limbo. Waves of restaurants are expected to close as they grapple with the problem of feeding people sitting in close proximity. Our culture of going down to the pub for a drink or dining out is history for the moment; how many will reopen is anybody's guess.

The whole world, it seems, is chasing face masks, reports *Guardian* writer Samantha Subramanian.

She says that epidemiologists have spoken highly of N95 respirators, masks that filter out 95 per cent of small particulate matter, and now entrepreneurs the world over are chasing them down. One man began phoning N95 suppliers in Mexico, Turkey, Indonesia, Ireland. Each one turned him down. "The answers ranged from 'No' to 'We only sell to accredited buyers' to 'Come back next year.' After three days, he found a South African company named North Safety Products, which had 500,000 masks in stock, and he bought them all, at less than a pound per mask, certain that he would be able to sell the surplus.

During their conversations, North Safety Products executives warned the buyer to be careful. There were 'interested parties' lurking outside its factory gates, ready to bribe truck drivers for their cargoes. So the buyer hired a security detail to ride alongside his truck of masks as it drove to the airport in Johannesburg. Six grim men, packing pistols and rifles, clad in camouflage and bulletproof vests. "They asked if I wanted machine guns as well. I thought not. We're not invading Lesotho. Let's keep it reasonable," he said.

In mid-February, two weeks after he placed his order, his shipment touched down in Hong Kong. Within six hours, the buyers he had signed up had collected nearly all of the masks. "Even if I'd had five million masks," he said, "I'd have sold out."

Some countries have hoarded masks, and used them as chips in geopolitical games. Thieves have made off with them. The fashion houses Prada, Gucci and Balenciaga have started to manufacture them.

Last year, a fashion industry insider said that Burberry had toyed with the notion of putting face masks on some of its models during a catwalk show – a wink, perhaps, at our apocalyptic future. By March, things had become real, and the fashion house has pledged to make masks and gowns for the UK's NHS. From a healthcare perspective, the mask was a matter of life and death. But in the fashion world it had already taken on the function of a talisman – as an object to hang comfortingly between the body and a diseased society.

And all of this, when we are still not clear on the advice about whether masks are helpful in stopping the virus spreading.

There are glimmers of hope. New Zealand is going back to work today, having stemmed the spread of the virus. Its Prime Minister, Jacinda Ardern, has played a blinder. A Nobel Prize may well be in the pipeline.

Australia says it had only 12 new cases of the virus over the past day. More than 2.4m people have downloaded a tracking app, as the country seeks to move into a new phase.

US President Donald Trump once again censured China's handling of the virus, saying: "We are not happy with China."

I'm sure that's true. But if Covid-19 costs Trump his hoped-for re-election in November, we will have China and the virus to thank for that. It will have been far too high a price to pay in terms of lost lives and economic ruin, but a lesson to us all that politics is a serious business, to which clowns and incompetents should not be invited.

I pick up the binoculars to check on Callum, who seems content under his rain rug, head down, munching. It's my turn to cook, and so I plan the day's meals – chicken sandwiches with mayo for lunch (from last night's roast chicken) and chops for supper with a salad. Nobody is going hungry in this house, which in time may be a problem. But so much less of a problem than those starving on London's streets.

Others, elsewhere, are starving too. My thoughts fly south to my wise, kind and funny sister Jay, making sandwiches three times a week to be distributed to desperately hungry children and adults in the townships of the Cape flats.

The dead are not the only victims of this virus, there are the hungry, the bereaved, the battered women – and our tattered, worthless politics.

CHAPTER 23

30th April 2020

Nurse Colleen O'Reilly tells it like it is

Seven weeks in lockdown does strange things to your mind. Even though we can hardly complain of cabin fever, I have started to think of things I would like to do and places to go when this mad time is over.

I have two stents in my heart and should be good for some years, though that could change in a heartbeat, not to put too fine a point on it. If I got Coronavirus, there would be little chance of my surviving it. So in these past weeks of peace and creativity, each day has been a reprieve from the Grim Reaper, and all the sweeter for that. Near on 43,000 people in the UK have died to date, while I have been given the gift of continued life. And that does something to you.

It has helped me to prioritise, for one thing. And I am beginning to think that if I do survive this pandemic, I would like to do something of a lap around my old and most beloved haunts, to walk in those landscapes that have meant the most to me. To say thank you to the gods for sparing me, in those places that have entered my soul and my heart, though the latter has become a somewhat crowded space.

As I lay in bed these last few nights of April, my mind has taken me out of this 260-year-old cottage for a mental

Cook's Tour of my special places across Europe and southward to South Africa and the Cape.

In Europe, there are two destinations, France and Greece, that matter most to me. I am sure that I am not alone in this urge to travel again. The punch-drunk airlines are going to be overwhelmed with travellers who have new life-work balance priorities, heading for the Mediterranean when all this is over. And for me, that means the Greek islands.

Everyone has their favourite Greek island. Ours is Skopelos. In the mid-1980s, we started to explore our new continent and fell in love with this island. It's not hard to do. And with us, it was love at first sight. The heat, the quality of the light and on Skopelos, that combination of green trees and turquoise sea, takes your breath away. Skopelos phonetically translated into my mother-tongue, Afrikaans, means to kick free. Indeed, the name proved prophetic.

We returned, year on year; eventually we brought our children to the island and Skopelos found a place in our family narrative. Today, its food informs our cooking, its sunshine and beauty inhabits our hearts and memories. It lies there at the top of the Aegean, waiting still, as it has through history – an emerald set in a sapphire sea. And we know that one day we will return, no longer young, somewhat hurt by life, and less romantic, and the island will beguile us again, for it is all it ever was, but now it is also family, part of us.

If I make it through the pandemic, I intend to walk and swim once more from the beaches of Skopelos, the perfect place to celebrate life.

Yesterday it was announced with some fanfare that Boris has become a father for the sixth time (we think; there may be others we don't know of yet). His fiancée, Carrie Symonds, produced a boy. Jacob Rees Mogg, the 'MP for the 18th Century' as he is known, complimented Boris for joining that most exclusive club at Westminster – those MPs who have six children. It is perhaps no wonder that The Mogg needs to recline on those green parliamentary benches in the way he does, from time to time.

On Twitter, a social commentator, Amicus Curiae,

says: "If a man had seven kids with three or four different women, having left his wife and mother of his children for a younger woman, and had an affair with an assortment of women, and then had a child with his much younger girlfriend, he might grace the Jeremy Kyle Show, not be our Prime Minister."

How do the British public put up with this Prime Minister and at the same time donate millions to Captain Tom Moore? Are we confused? I suspect we are. Captain Tom turns 100 today, having raised £30m for NHS charities, and has received some 125,000 birthday cards from around the world. He is awarded the honorary rank of Colonel by the British Army. He has tried to remind us that the NHS is funded by the taxpayer; it is not a charity.

But it's not all happiness and reward today in Britain. A heartbroken nurse, Colleen O'Reilly, blogs about the central drama of this time, writing of the death from Covid-19 of a 55-year-old man, a patient in her hospital, who like thousands of others, passed away without a human touch. She brings us bedside to a drama that has been repeated tens of thousands of times this past two months. It is almost inconceivable. Colleen, we grieve with you and for you. I quote her words here in full:

She says: "It's my third week as a nurse on a COVID unit and I'm gonna say it, I am not OK. I typically can handle almost anything. I'm usually not vulnerable like this, let alone on social media, but I must share my experience, particularly my past few days."

"Wednesday night I took care of the most grateful and appreciative 55-year-old man. Thursday morning he called me into the room to promise him I would order him something other than eggs for breakfast and laughed with me when he randomly explained his hatred for white rice lol. I was tidying the room and talking with him, until literally right in front of my eyes, he was gasping for air and needed to go from a very minimal amount of oxygen to a non-rebreather (a lot of oxygen). When I went to work last night, I unfortunately wasn't taking care of him but saw his nurse working her ass off as he wasn't doing well. Overnight, this man required the highest amount of oxygen that someone could be on without being intubated. By 6:45am he was struggling to breathe, even with that high amount of oxygen, and within 30 minutes we watched his oxygen levels quickly drop and his heart begin to slow down.

"As a nurse, I truly take pride in being with someone as they take their last breath. I really believe it is an honour to be beside them during their last moments of life. This was SO different. When this man took his last breath, I cried. NOT because he died…but because although there were three of us in the room with him – he truly died alone. I swear, I am SO grateful for the PPE we are given at this hospital but I have never in my life felt less of a human than when I have it on. Solely because I am not allowed to touch my patients…even if they are dying. We were in the room, but you can barely tell that there is a person underneath our Tyvek suits, and as badly as I wanted to take my gloves off just to hold his hand, I couldn't. I am disgusted, looking at this photo of me, knowing that this is what my patients see when I take care of them.

"I'm not sure I'm accurately putting into words how I feel, but I pray to God that no one ever feels that way. This man wasn't supposed to die. He especially wasn't supposed to die isolated from humans or the human touch. We are required to wear these full suits for our whole shift, the rooms have no windows, and there are no visitors allowed in the hospital. This patient came to the hospital six days ago. That means that he has not physically seen a human or touched a human for the full six days before he died. I will never get over that.

"Truthfully, I will gladly be the doctor's eyes when they can't physically be there. I will happily be my patient's voice when they can't be their own. I will be EVS, respiratory, transport, phlebotomy. I will be my patient's daughter, granddaughter, best friend, therapist… whatever shoes they need me to fill. But I am not a machine.

"Patients are not animals, and healthcare workers are not robots. If you are blessed enough to be able to self-quarantine, **PLEASE DO**. I can only speak for myself but the people I am seeing die, are not supposed to be dying. These people are not just a number on TV during this pandemic and nurses are not machines. There is only so much we can handle – so please spare us some time to figure this out. Stay home, and God bless."

Reading this, my mind recoils from the horror of it, and my heart goes out to this wonderful human being, Colleen O'Reilly, who writes so bravely about what most of us are so lucky not to see or have to deal with. As you were in that room Colleen, he did not die alone.

I spoke to my brother last night. He is once more in San Francisco, loading Fedex trucks with nitrile gloves from China and waiting for a load of masks next week. I ask him again why he is doing this, putting his life on the line for his employer, and he says his hope is to save lives and also to help keep the company he works for alive for all its workers. He is a remarkable and courageous man.

And I think too of all the medical staff and frontline workers around the world, who are daily drawing on their reserves of courage. Thank you!

CHAPTER 24

1st May 2020

Boris and the three little pigs

Today is May 1st, and the emergency callsign 'MayDay, MayDay, MayDay' has never seemed more appropriate. Much of the news is about how and when the lockdown will end here in the UK. Boris is due to outline a plan this week. A survey just out says that Britain has been self-isolating, not because the Government demanded it, but because people were truly fearful of catching the virus and even when lockdown is lifted, many would be nervous of leaving their homes to use public transport, visit pubs, or go shopping.

If and when Boris lifts lockdown, let's see how soon the general population take up the offer of walking out through their front door. It will be a telling indication of how much Boris is viewed as being capable of making a judgement call that anyone can trust. I am reminded of the wolf and the three little pigs. The pigs are cowering in their house as the wolf calls out in a falsetto voice. "Oh little pigs it is safe to come out now, the big bad wolf is gone!" I think Boris has a profound credibility problem.

His mate across the pond, US President Donald Trump, has announced that he has seen compelling evidence that the virus was manufactured in a Wuhan laboratory in China. What he is unsure of is whether it escaped accidentally or whether it was deliberately allowed to spread. But US Government experts say the virus is "not manmade or genetically modified." Oh Lord! Trump will leave the White House today for the first time in a month when he travels to the Camp David presidential retreat in Maryland. For how long, nobody is sure.

The UK Government is sticking to its figure of 26,000 dead in hospitals and nursing homes but not yet at home, a far cry from the 43,000 *The Financial Times* and the Office of National Statistics have mentioned.

There is concern that Boris's right hand man, Dominic Cummings, the architect of his political victories with Brexit and the general election, his 'eminence grise', has been attending SAGE, the scientific body set up to guide the Government. The fear is that as a result, the scientists are not at liberty to talk freely, and that their messages to Government are being edited by Cummings.

The weather has turned cold and wet for three days now, much closer to the seasonal norm after the warmest April ever recorded. Lockdown has largely been a case of being indoors while the sun shone outside. And this after the wettest winter in living memory, when people were desperate for a bit of sun.

A new study shows that 18 to 24-year-olds have been hardest hit by lockdown, coping worst with its confining realities. It makes sense, with hormones in full flow and the sap rising in spring, that they are going stir-crazy. It will be interesting to see when lockdown ends, how soon they start circulating, choosing sex over the fear of death. My bet is that Death won't get much attention from them, unless Death starts paying them particular attention himself. And I suppose that this youthful brio is the way of the world and just how we as a species have bounced back from worse setbacks than this hiccup.

It was so good to see Dom and Steph yesterday, however briefly. Both Jan and I were so much wanting to to hug them, to kiss them. To be with them and to embrace them. To thank them for all they have done for us. Yesterday they popped in to collect their post and their parcels delivered here, to take Gus to the vet for his annual shots and to do some top-up shopping for us. They looked well and happy and full of life and in love. Their lockdown in Jupiter's tiny confines has not challenged their relationship at all. It is not surprising, as the 37 ft yacht has been a dream boat for them, helping them to realise their ambition of a life afloat, carrying them round Britain's treacherous coast safely in the first leg of the new life they have planned for themselves.

Through the dark days of winter and then the bright sunny days of lockdown, they have been studying for their captain's tickets. While the world has been locked down, these two have focused on how to navigate the earth by the stars. It is no wonder that they have coped. They have been travelling the heavens, even as Britain feared to open its front door; their shared dream of going further and faster across the world's oceans is gaining strength, day by day.

During this dark time, they have put together a compelling business plan to buy a bigger boat to run a charter service for university oceanographic departments, and have done a lot of research to this end. They have spoken to universities about what their requirements would be in the way of yacht chartering for their scientific teams. And just before lockdown, they flew to New Zealand to view three yachts.

Now they have come up with a new strand of their plan. Both aim to study further. Dominic has opted to study boat building – marine architecture – and Steph, who is a chemical engineer, to study marine biology. This part of our family are truly leaving the land for the sea. And that part of me that loves the sea is singing for joy, while at the same time my fear and respect for the sea gives me pause. Please God keep them safe as they sail upon the earth's oceans and come to harbour in good heart, each time they leave port. They already make a formidable team, their courage and spirit of adventure wedded to intelligence and discipline. I am so very proud of them. Their children one day will be Vikings!

But before any of this can happen, we need to beat Covid-19; that is the storm we are all riding at anchor, and it is fairly tossing our British barque about.

Yesterday afternoon Jan drove me to collect my car from our mechanic in Groombridge, ten minutes from home. Then in rubber gloves, having sprayed the car seat and steering wheel, I drove my old car back home through Crowborough. It felt good to be moving again in this car that I am so fond of, a car that has criss-crossed Europe with us for thousands of miles, eating the distances effortlessly, in effect our home from home. I will have to keep the battery charged by giving it an outing regularly from now on. Diesels thrive on work.

It tickles me no end that in the TV series we've been watching, *Ray Donovan,* the character after whom the series is named, drives the same car as me. His son says he too wants to be a gangster like his father, and when his mother denies that her husband is a gangster, he says: "Mom, look at the way dad dresses, look at his car!" Maybe at heart I am a gangster too? Maybe.

And speaking of bad behaviour, Britain's largest pharmacy chain, Boots, is now supporting domestic abuse victims. They will be able to access safe spaces at Boots pharmacies across the country from today, under measures to improve access to support during the Coronavirus lockdown.

These stories of how the virus is infecting our lives have no end. One that catches my eye in *The Guardian* is about failed ventilators. "Chinese ventilators that ministers heralded as vital to the NHS's efforts to tackle Covid-19 were badly built, unsuitable for use in hospitals and potentially dangerous for patients, it has emerged."

All of the devices in a consignment of 250 ventilators that arrived from China on April 4 posed such serious problems that they could not be used and were ditched. Doctors in NHS hospitals in the West Midlands, among which the ventilators were shared, were so concerned that they wrote to Matt Hancock the health secretary, warning that they could kill patients.

"We believe that if used, significant patient harm, including death, is likely," they wrote in a letter, which was obtained by NBC News. "We look forward to the withdrawal and replacement of these ventilators with devices better able to provide intensive care ventilation for our patients."

However, as they say, the darkest hour is just before the dawn, and there are glimmers of light on the horizon. The Government says that the country has now achieved its stated target of testing 100,000 people a day, many of these at drive-through facilities run by the army. And now a key test is underway. A randomly selected group of 100,000 people in England will be tested for Covid-19 in an attempt to quantify whether transmission levels of the virus are low enough to exit the lockdown. The tests, next week, will provide a national snapshot of the proportion of those infected with the virus ahead of a planned review of restrictions on May 7.

Professor Ara Darzi, the director of the Institute of Global Health Innovation at Imperial College London, which is running the study with the pollster Ipsos Mori, said that – short of a vaccine – testing represented the only way out of the lockdown. "But the testing landscape is like the Wild West with no rules, no standards and widely varying reliability," he added. "With this ambitious programme, the biggest in England, we aim to establish a viable testing programme on which the Government can rely."

Amen to that!

In South Africa, which has a draconian lockdown, one of the toughest in the world, they have managed to limit deaths to just over 103, according to official figures. This has been achieved with stringent lockdown measures and an army of social care workers going through townships testing and testing and testing for Covid-19. But the fear now is that this strategy may be hurting the country more than the virus.

South Africa's lockdown is costing its ailing economy £570 million a day. Yet with fewer than 103 dead and just 395 infected patients in hospital, the country's population is beginning to question if that has been a price worth paying. A phased easing of restrictions, starting tomorrow, will offer some relief but there are fears that the number of failed businesses and job losses will be far higher than the number of fatalities from Covid-19.

"Even if our unlikely hopes of escaping the health consequences of the pandemic come to pass, we will not escape its economic consequences," Ravi Naidoo, an expert on development policy, said.

Amid all the gloom, there is the odd story to make one smile. Here in the UK, the mainstay of celebration is beer, and today brings heartening news. It sounds like an offer that drinkers anywhere would raise a glass to – a brewery is giving away its beer after being left with a surplus amid lockdown. With pubs and restaurants closed, the firm was left with nobody to sell its dozens of casks to.

The Alnwick Brewery Company in Northumberland has asked local residents to take its cask beer home in their own containers. In return, they were requested to make a donation that will go to the NHS.

The brewery said one person "joked he would arrive with a bathtub." Each cask holds about 70 pints (some 40 litres).

"We'd brewed up in anticipation of Easter. Suddenly the business was shut down and we thought: "What can we do with this?" co-owner Ian Robinson said. "It's all very well giving it away, but why not try to raise some money through donations?" The beer has a relatively short lifespan, and we're down to its last three weeks, so we'll be doing this for the next few Fridays."

We can expect a rush north to Northumberland for a cask or two for the weekend.

And then there is happy news from my connections in South Africa. My sister Jay in Cape Town sends news: "Just back from our first walk in five weeks! We are allowed out between 6am and 9am. We went along the roads – me in an engineered sock mask! Everyone very festive and all saying hello." I am glad for her and Guy.

Elma in Johannesburg writes: "Went for a long walk to freedom this morning as it is now allowed. Hurrah. Good to breathe again." And she attaches an image of a magnificent tree with a vast trunk from which massive branches reach out just five feet from the ground. And I am happy for her too.

Small steps to freedom for us all.

CHAPTER 25

1st May 2020

A new Pharoah gets a kicking from a modern Moses

As usual, I keep an eye on how things are going in both South Africa and California and this morning I get an interesting heads-up about South Africa's President getting a kicking.

François, a South African friend based in Kent, forwards the following, saying: "Bit dramatic, but it sums up the vibe in SA." It is an email sent to the South African President, Cyril Ramaphosa by Gareth Cliff, a radio and TV personality whose shows air on Jacaranda FM and News 24 among others.

It reads:

"Dear President Ramaphosa

I'm going to keep this brief, because I know you're dealing with a lot:

We've all been ready to support you and your administration in your efforts to save lives from this pandemic. Even people like me, who have questioned the idea of a lockdown as the best response, have decided to comply and do whatever we could to help. We set aside our concerns over the heavy-handedness of the police and army; we swallowed and accepted that poor people in informal housing would be crammed into their one-room dwellings for a month; we limited our trips to the shops and even accepted not being able to buy hot food (for whatever inexplicable reason).

When you couldn't put your mask on, we laughed and we were charmed to see that you were able to laugh at yourself too. For a time, you won everyone over again. You yourself have said that it has taken much for people to give up their liberties, their right to be with family and friends and the ability to freely move around. Our patience and emotional state of affairs are on a knife-edge. We are losing hope.

Governments walk a fine line in times like these, where the regulations not only have to make sense, but also have to have significant buy-in from the public — otherwise people will break them, in big ways and small. South Africans are mostly compliant — but when you promise something and then break that promise, it makes us feel like we should break your regulations in return.

Many of us aren't afraid of the virus anymore. It's our health, and we'll take our chances, thank you. We ARE afraid of the havoc your lockdown is wreaking on the economy, on people's lives and livelihoods. I see fewer and fewer explanations from ministers and more and more capricious, some would say spiteful, regulation. I'm not a smoker — I don't like cigarettes at all — but when Minister Dlamini-Zuma announced that she was (after a consultation none of us believe happened) going to keep the ban on tobacco products in place, many of us (even the non-smokers) were ready to give her the middle finger — and start risking breaking the rules. There are more of us than there are police officers and soldiers, so if you piss enough people off, things get very hairy. I'm sure those advisers in the security cluster have mentioned that they can't shoot us all or put us all in jail.

Your Government, Sir, have not covered themselves in glory over the last 10 years. Some people in this country already have a taste of anarchy, where municipalities are bankrupt and there is no service delivery. They see no evidence that the ANC will fix parastatals, cronyism, kleptocracy and for once and for all cease their childish flirtation with outdated and failed socialist ideas. Your hold on power depends on people willing to comply with the rules – the same rules they expect you to comply with. Our patience grows thin, and in tandem your tax collection runs dry. When you speak of a social compact, it goes both ways. You have to take your boot off our throats.

When Moses told Pharaoh to let his people go, Pharaoh didn't listen and there were plagues. We all know how that story went for Pharaoh. You have to start letting our people go Mr President, or this plague will be the least of our worries. Even Moses would tell you that.

Yours,
Gareth Cliff'

Oh Lord! It cannot be easy being Cyril Ramaphosa right now, picking up from the ruination left by his predecessor Jacob Zuma with all the corrupt political machine still largely in place, economic devastation all around and now Covid-19 with very few tools either human or financial to deal with this latest threat. Who'd be a politician right now? I think President Ramaphosa has made a decent start, given the cards he holds, and has gained some respect for his statesmanship, but there will always be naysayers. I wonder what Mr Cliff would be saying if South Africa had Britain's death toll? And it's still very early days in South Africa's Covid-19 experience. It could get ugly.

It has been a bizarre day, weatherwise; we've had

three mini-storms pass through with sunshine between. After lunch, Jan and I decided to have a walk down the hill to see the bluebells. As we came out of our drive, a small grey Renault pulled up. It was Georgie, the groom who is looking after Callum. She said that he has been behaving himself on their walks down to his paddock, so much so that she takes her own horse, Claude, at the same time, walking the two large warmbloods to pasture. There was however, a 'BUT'. Two days ago Callum got the wind under his tail and decided to take off for his field, almost tearing the lead-rope out of Georgie's hand. But Georgie, though not tall, is no pushover. She hung on for grim death and managed to control the huge 17hh chestnut with both hands, letting Claude loose. Claude, to his eternal credit, just kept walking by her side. Callum, she said, was not best pleased to be thwarted in his bid for freedom, and made faces.

As we headed downhill into the woods, the sky to the west turned an ominous black. At first, the thunder was muted, but then the rain started softly, and by the time we reached the valley floor, the storm was overhead with lashing rain, thunder and lightning. Gus was totally unperturbed. And then it began to hail just as we reached the bluebells.

We sheltered under the trees, with our jacket hoods up over our caps, and stood, heads down like old horses, watching the mossy ground underfoot turn white with hail. As it eased off, we saw a figure appear out of the mist, a neighbour of ours, Susie and her Labradoodle Stanley, a large, white, curly haired lad, coming down the track heading to their home in the woods nearby. We were guests of hers and her husband Ed at Christmas, which seems like a lifetime ago, not just four months. Stanley stood like a good 'un. He was a total teenage tearaway who used to jump on Gus when out walking, but is now a rather sedate gent of a dog. Gus was not entirely convinced, and stood tight against my leg.

As we headed home, we passed the bridge where long ago we hid clues to a treasure hunt for a friend's young daughters to find. At my age, time ricochets back and forth, the present, the past, the distant past. Facing the steep climb up the hill to the cottage, my memory canters back to a scene at this very spot that still makes me smile even now.

Some years ago, I was riding home on Chancer, a lovely dappled grey Irish Draught, who I bought as an unbroken three-year-old and who turned into a great riding horse who was unusually good on the forest at night under moonlight.

As I pointed him up the hill for a last run home, I noticed a bunch of young cyclists on mountain bikes, pelting down the hill at a great lick. The lead rider spotted me and yelled over his shoulder to his friends in Afrikaans: *"Oppas! Daar is 'n ou toppie op 'n perd!"* (Careful! There's an old codger on a horse!) I could not resist – as they came level with me, having slowed right down, I in turn shouted out: *"Wie de hel is jou ou toppie?"* (Who the hell is your old codger?) There was a stunned silence, and then we all started laughing at the same time. We chatted for a while and it turned out they were down from London for the day for a spot of countryside enjoyment. We spoke briefly of South Africa and I told them I was from Cape Town and had lived here for decades. As ever with fellow South Africans, there was an instant connection, and as I wished them well and rode up the hill slowly now, tears in my eyes and a bit choked by the warmth and *menslikheid* (humanity) of the conversation, thinking of all I had lost.

Back home from our walk, once more in the present, Jan planned a delicious supper, having had a food delivery earlier – steak and asparagus with baked potatoes. I put my feet up with a bag of salt and vinegar crisps, and listened to the BBC for the news of the day.

Currently the search for a vaccine is in the forefront of all minds. The first human trial for a vaccine was announced last month by scientists in Seattle. Unusually, they are skipping any animal research to test its safety or effectiveness. In Oxford, the first human trial in Europe has started with more than 800 recruits. Pharmaceutical giants Sanofi and GSK have teamed up to develop a vaccine.

And this floored me: Australian scientists have begun

injecting ferrets with two potential vaccines. It is the first comprehensive pre-clinical trial involving animals, and the researchers hope to test humans by the end of April. Ferrets? How strange.

However, no one knows how effective any of these vaccines will be. My bet is that Australian Bruces and Sheilas will thrive on the ferret serum, but it may not cure us all.

CHAPTER 26
2nd May 2020

Early talk of ending lockdown in Europe

Tomorrow, May 3, is 'International Dawn Chorus Day'. People across Britain are urged by BBC Radio 4's *Farming Today* programme to get up early to hear the avian orchestra tune up from 4.30am for the earth's greatest symphony, led by robins and blackbirds, which are usually first out of their nests. This glorious sound, which wakes me each morning of lockdown, is in its way a sex-led frenzy as birds call to seek a mate and to claim breeding-feeding territory as their own.

I wonder how this behaviour would play out if it was part of the human range? Perish the thought; we have enough issues as a species ourselves.

British newspapers report today that France has been told that its exit strategy from lockdown hinges on 'red and green' regions and mass testing. The French have said they will begin to strip back confinement measures on May 11. France will start gradually easing lockdown to avoid economic collapse in a week's time, but tighter restrictions will remain in 'red' regions, Paris and the North East, which have high infection levels. The country could backtrack if the epidemic flares up again, warned the French prime minister, Édouard

Philippe. He told Parliament the decision to confine the population to their homes six weeks ago had saved 62,000 lives, but it was now time to start lifting the lockdown to avoid economic collapse. France has been one of the hardest-hit countries in Europe, with more than 20,000 deaths thus far. "We are going to have to learn to live with Covid-19 and to protect ourselves from it," he said. "It is a fine line that must be followed. A little too much carelessness, and the epidemic restarts. A little too much caution, and the entire country sinks."

Spain has announced it hopes to return to 'normality' by the end of June.

As I write, more than half of humanity is under some sort of lockdown to stem the spread of the pandemic. But with some countries reporting falling infection numbers, governments are beginning to chart their way out of the shutdowns that have pummelled the global economy.

These plans to lift lockdown are to go ahead despite the rise in German Covid-19 infection rates after its own relaxation of restrictions.

Here in the UK, we are waiting till next week to hear what Boris has planned for the lifting of our own lockdown.

In the US, a drug is being made available which is said to inhibit the growth of Covid-19 and has proved effective in some patients. US regulators have allowed the emergency use of the experimental drug Remdesivir, which appears to help some Coronavirus patients recover faster. It is the first drug shown to help fight Covid-19, which has killed more than 230,000 people worldwide, as of today. Donald Trump announced the news on Friday at the White House alongside Stephen Hahn, the Food and Drug Administration (FDA) commissioner, who said the drug would be available for patients hospitalised with Covid-19.

The emergency approval comes days after Dr Anthony Fauci, the Government's top infectious disease expert, expressed cautious optimism about the results of a Remdesivir drug trial. "The data shows that Remdesivir has a clear-cut, significant, positive effect in diminishing the time to recovery," Fauci said earlier this week. "What it has proven is that a drug can block this virus."

The UK hasn't been shaking as much since it went into Covid lockdown. This is a story that catches my eye in *The Guardian*. Seismometer stations, which are normally used to record earthquakes, have detected a big fall in the ground vibrations linked to human activity. Scientists from Imperial College London say this background hum is now half what it would usually be.

The unprecedented seismic quiet – a phenomenon mirrored in other countries – could offer a unique opportunity to study the Earth's interior. "You'd have to go back decades to see noise levels like this," commented Imperial's Dr Stephen Hicks. "You'd often get quiet times in the evenings or at weekends but not continuously, for weeks," he told BBC News.

Human activity – cars, lorries, trains, industry, and footfall – turn up in seismometers in a band of frequencies from 5 to 15 Hertz. Dr Hicks used the data from 127 instruments spread across Britain to map the signal's evolution from mid-January to the present. He relied in part on the high-fidelity scientific stations operated by the British Geological Survey, but also on a network of citizen science seismometers.

The vibrations sensed in both sets of instruments were seen to drop off dramatically after Prime Minister Boris Johnson ordered Britain into lockdown on March 23. "The reduction in seismic noise should help us to see signals from earthquakes that are normally buried in the noise," said Dr Brian Baptie, the head of seismology at the BGS.

How is that for a silver lining? Or is it golden, as in silence?

Soon British commuters could be asked to take their temperature before leaving home as part of proposals to make public transport safer. It is understood to be among measures being considered for when the Coronavirus lockdown is eased. A fever with a temperature above 37.8 Centigrade is one of the two main symptoms of the virus, the other being a dry, continuous cough.

Having commuted from Sussex to London for years, I can only wonder at this new hurdle facing hard-pressed commuters. Before wrestling with the joys of British Rail, millions will have to start their day with a thermometer. That thought is enough to raise one's temperature.

And I notice an interesting crack developing in the British Government's hardline Brexit stance, reported in *The Guardian*.

"The British Government is quietly seeking access to the European Union's pandemic warning system, despite early reluctance to cooperate on health after Brexit, *The Guardian* has learned." Now there is a surprise – or maybe not!

The UK is seeking "something akin to membership" of the EU's early warning and response system (EWRS), which has played a critical role in coordinating Europe's response to the Coronavirus, as well as to earlier pandemics such as bird flu. According to an EU source, this would be "pretty much the same" as membership of the EU system.

As a committed 'Remainer' who voted to keep Britain in the EU, I smile wryly reading this, and wonder how many other aspects of the EU Boris will quietly be trying to ease back into?

Russia, too, is having its own battle with the virus. Two per cent of Moscow's residents are infected, says its Mayor – some 250,000 people. According to official stastistics, Moscow has a population of 12.7 million people, but the real figure is believed to be higher.

Moscow has significantly increased testing capacity over the past few weeks, and the city has managed to contain the spread of the infection due to the enforcement of stay-at-home rules and other measures, say the authorities.

And something practical and light-hearted out of China today. To help remind kids of the importance of social distancing amid the pandemic, one school in Hangzhou has its young students wearing special headwear to class. The hats were all designed and made by the students themselves (presumably with a bit of help from their parents) before returning to school this week. Each hat includes a kind of rotor blade, a metre long, made of every conceivable material from plastic to cardboard, to long skinny balloons, which helps to remind the kids to keep their distance from each other as they create a one-metre buffer zone around each of the first- to third-graders.

My thoughts this morning turn to our own plans for the day. Cleaning the house is on the cards, not a prospect I relish, but Gus fluff is evident everywhere. Jan gave him a shower this morning as he stank to high heaven after the vets cleared his blocked anal glands, an excuse if ever there was one not to be a vet. Poor Gus was somewhat bewildered and downcast over the past two days by not being allowed on couches or beds. So now he smells pretty good and hopefully won't be doing his butt-wipe arse-drag walk on the lawn. And the house needs cleaning.

By way of thanking Jan for doing the heavy lifting on Gus, I make American style pancakes for breakfast, slathered in honey, raspberries and Greek yogurt, with some fried Chorizo sausage on the side for some salt and spice, as we are out of bacon.

We then take the newly clean Gus for a trip to see Callum and Traveller and have a walk through the bluebells, as they won't last much longer with all the rain we've had. Both horses are fine, Callum in for the day as his field is sodden after yesterday's downpour, but Traveller is happy as a clam in his field and rolls over twice in the mud to make the point.

After a sandwich lunch, I do some reading and then weed the garden, pulling out thistles and stinging nettles and that sticky green climbing plant that given rein will take over a whole bed. And I tie up the climbing roses which have tipped over from the wall in our last storm. The weather is still very mixed, sunshine and cloud alternating.

Our day ends quietly with supper and a movie, and I make a mental note to be up early for 'International Dawn Chorus Day' tomorrow. Things in Britain cannot be that desperate if thousands of people across the land will rise with the lark tomorrow to listen to birdsong.

CHAPTER 27

3rd May 2020

Dawn Chorus Day

What a morning chorus it is on this International Dawn Chorus Day. I wake at 5.20am and listen, as one solitary bird takes centre stage against a soft background chorus. I wish I knew what it is, but sadly don't. To me, it sounds like the rolling silver tinkling trills of the caged canaries my father kept in his bedroom; it is an impassioned song, that seems to last minutes on end without a break. The bird creates its own 'wall of sound', much like the effect that made the name of record producer Phil Spector, who was found guilty, years after the fame it brought him, of murdering actress Lana Clarkson. (In the days ahead I record the sound of this bird and discover from ornithologist and author Tim Dee that it is the song of a wren, a bird he describes as "Small but mighty. An energetic walnut.")

My morning minstrel sings on and on, and I sleep again. I wake once more at eight this Sunday morning and go down for coffee. I am glad to have found myself among an audience of millions listening to the bird concert, uniting us all, despite being locked down in our homes. Thank God for song.

And then, by one of those uncanny coincidences, I

turn on the radio, and the first item I hear on BBC Radio 4's *Sunday* programme is that Germany plans to reopen its churches for regular services, but there will be no singing allowed. The hymns, I imagine, will have to be internal. I wonder how the Germans will take to that; with discipline and good humour, I suppose.

I don't feel that great today, despite the wonders of the dawn chorus. My knees ache from our recent walks, and my energy levels are down. Instinctively, I breathe deep, testing my lungs. They seem fine, but I am losing fitness, as I am not currently responsible for looking after Callum, mucking out and riding each day. One more month of this lockdown will leave me with unwanted weight gain. It's a fine judgment call, but I think I need to return to my normal schedule as soon as lockdown ends.

I drag myself away from these depressing thoughts, and look through some photos I took of the spectacular rhododendrons over on the Forest yesterday when we went to visit Traveller. They are like a 15-foot wave of hot pink crashing onto the green turf. They are a reminder of Britain's empire, when explorers and botanists brought every conceivable kind of plant back to Britain from every corner of the world in the 18th century. The Rhododendrons came from northern India, the high country near the Himalayas I believe, and today they grace so many British gardens. They are the national flower of Nepal. I think of them as Britain's equivalent of South Africa's bougainvillea; a Mardi Gras Fiesta of hot reds and pinks with occasional white, cream and yellow. Two strange names, rhododendrons and bougainvillea. And speaking of strange names…

Boris and Carrie have named their son Wilfred Lawrie Nicholas, after his two grandfathers, and the doctors who saved Boris's life, who were both called Nick. Dear God! What are the chances of the lad calling himself Wilfred when he gets to 15 years of age?

And thinking of age and change, it has not passed my own internal clock that from today I have a fortnight to go till I reach the grand old age of 70. How did that happen? I had certainly not planned on it, and yet here I am, haunted by the horror of Covid-19, very much wanting to make it to my birthday without falling ill or dying. Why? But something in me says 70 is a better innings than 69. It does not leave you looking quite so short-changed. Sixty-nine may have its raffish supporters, but 70 has more gravitas.

Just recently, I helped to spread the ashes of our 90-year old friend, Simone Deschamps, under a rowan tree on Ashdown Forest. Simone, who had been so desperate to cross the Styx for the two years since her dog died. Age has very little to recommend it. It's a bitch, and yet, and yet, we cling onto life for fear of something worse.

It is such a strange business, this business of age. If you are lucky and you are in reasonably good physical and mental shape, there are still pleasures to be had, for sure. The beauty of the earth, the warmth of the sun, the company of one's children and grandchildren if they still speak to you. There are books and art and beauty, there is food and wine and travel. But there is also a cruel reality: you need to master new things, among them humility and caution.

You have to be consciously cautious all the time of the danger of falling over, and humble in the face of needing help for a variety of things, or to be taken somewhere, once you can no longer drive. Or (if you are me) be shown how to manage airport check-ins or supermarket self-service check-outs.

And if you are a man, your relationship with half the world's population, women, changes too, it has to. What may once have been seen as charm or banter or even flirting are now unacceptable. Nobody wants to be seen as a dirty old man, so you edit everything you say, and work hard not to offend. You don't wish to appear ridiculous. And yet all those things you felt at 20 are still there, but those feelings have outlived their usefulness. Your romantic inclinations, your gallantry, are now a danger to you.

You worry as much about living as about dying. A major concern is money. Will you have enough money to see you through to the end in a manner to which you have become accustomed? Will you end up impoverished, under the roof of a relative who is not delighted with the deal? Or in a retirement home that gobbles up your diminishing assets and its residents, as we've seen in this age-focused pandemic?

I know Simone would have been delighted to find that suddenly she had a guaranteed one-way ticket out of her room in the care home. That said, this death by Covid-19 is not the 'Old Man's Friend', commonly used to describe pneumonia; it is an unspeakably horrible way to go.

Younger people ask if they may use your first name, and some don't even ask and use it anyway, which feels like a brutal loss of dignity. More dignity goes when you have to plan each trip and outing with toilets in mind.

Hair loss is never easy for any man and now it goes fast, and is replaced by hair sprouting from your ears and nose. A visit to the barber ends these days with a candle flame held to your ears to singe the hairs away – pretty alarming the first time it was done.

You forget the name of books and films and actors, sometimes even friends and acquaintances. And the fear of Alzheimer's haunts you. You struggle to keep up with ordering prescriptions, and each night struggle to open foil wrappers as you count out the handful needed to keep you alive.

There is not much good to be said for getting old.

We need to arrange things better at this end of life. People need to be able to control their own destinies and not need to drag themselves off to Switzerland when they want to call time on living. Each of us should be free to choose when we have reached the bus stop where we wish to alight from this journey. It would be a source of great comfort to have the means within your control to do that, to have a last meal with loved ones and then to bed, to sleep, to dream, never to wake, to pass into the great unknown of death at a time and place of your own choosing.

I certainly don't want to have bloody Covid-19 whip me off to a mass grave. Forgive my morbidity.

This downer comes at a strange time, because yester-

day was in fact a red-letter day for me; I received an unexpected gift from the universe, an early birthday present. And
a very special one indeed.

Late yesterday afternoon, I checked my email and
there was a message from Alec Hogg, the editor of BizNews
in South Africa. He said he would like to publish this journal,
a chapter each day. Reading his words, the world stilled, everything seemed to slow down and once again I felt that joy
that has meant so much to me, to have one's writing
acknowledged and to be published again.

Alec wrote: "Read the early chapters today and really
love the autobiographical style, gentle pace and beautiful writing. As a starting point, are you comfortable for us to
start with Ch1 and publish a chapter each day? If so, am
happy to kick off on Monday. Please confirm so that I can
start to set it up."

I am so moved I can hardly move. It is 16 years since
my last book *Boerejood* was published. A very busy and eventful
decade and a half, in which I did not find the time or space to
write creatively for myself. And now this.

I have been in touch with Maggie Davey and Bridget
Impey, my publishers at Jacana in Johannesburg, to say that
Alec had expressed possible interest, and they were support-
ive. This is exactly how my first book, *A Fisherman in the Saddle*,
found a publisher in Jacana, by being serialised first in South
Africa's *Country Life* magazine.

I send word to my long-suffering sister Jay in Cape
Town, my first reader, who has been ploughing through these
pages from day one, just as she did for my first two books.
Her reaction is congratulatory, but wise owl that she is, she
warns: "There will be those who politically disagree with you.
Be prepared for both bouquets and brickbats." I know she is
right, but this book is motivated by my most profound beliefs,
and for once I have not finessed my feelings but tried to tell it
as I see it, warts and all.

Jan is delighted and offers to edit the book for me. She
is the best and most meticulous editor and helped my other
books greatly. I am grateful. As we walk Gus down the lane

before supper, she takes my arm in hers. "Happy?" she asks, smiling. As a writer and author herself, with three books to her name, she does not really have to ask. She knows.

CHAPTER 28
4th May 2020

The world is serenading itself in lockdown

My sister Jay in Cape Town sends me a video and press cuttings she knows I will enjoy, and which also turn a knife in my chest, the knife of homesickness and longing – *heimvee*. She knows me very well. And she has often encouraged me to make the move back home.

I have been sorely tempted, many times. The thought of walking those beloved beaches with her and Guy again is always a wonderful prospect. Cape friends, culture, humour and soul food still call loudly to me. Some day, Jan and I might take up that invitation, so that my ashes can lie on the slopes of Table Mountain, above my boyhood home.

This morning Jay sends a video of two women singers, Karen Zoid and a neighbour of hers, Zola, on a rooftop of a block of flats in Seapoint, Cape Town. They play a Yiddish-Afrikaans medley aimed at the Jewish and Afrikaans community of this cosmopolitan seaside suburb, who stand in the lit windows of their apartment blocks at dusk to hear this skyline concert.

And it stops me in my tracks, as the cultural mix is my exact heritage, and I've not seen it fused in this way ever before. When my Afrikaans Christian mother married my

Jewish father in the late 1940s, their union caused a huge ruckus on both sides of the family. My formidable Jewish grandmother, Esther, on being told of the wedding by one of her other sons, said: "If you had told me that Leon had died, I would be less upset." And on the actual wedding day, one of my mother's brothers-in-law, husband of her sister Mabel, cursed her for marrying a Jew, and once more, when she raised us, her children, in the Jewish faith, even though she never converted herself.

And yet here in 2020, two singers are celebrating a musical marriage between these two cultures. My Boerejood heart is full, listening to the music and my eyes are wet. What, I wonder, would my parents have said?

It has taken Covid-19 to bring this strange fusion together, the sounds of Russian shtetls and the African veld. The audience in the Seapoint flats stand by their brightly lit windows, rapt, listening. They may be locked down in one way, but are freed in another, to enjoy this cross-cultural celebration. Their shared story is one of two tribes who came from Europe centuries ago to make Africa their home, a challenge that makes a few weeks stuck at home seem like a tea party in comparison.

My brother Herman in California sends me a video of the country and western song, *Green Green Grass of Home*, shot against a Cape Town backdrop. And much as I fight it, there are tears in my eyes once more by the end of the song. I've been gone from my birthplace for 40 years, but my roots remain intact and the pull of that flat-topped mountain reaches me here in Sussex effortlessly and enters the stent-corrupted chambers of my heart all too easily.

This sharing of music in neighbourhoods around the world is one of the bittersweet symbols of this time. From opera sung on Italian balconies to Yiddish songs sung in Cape Town, the world is singing to its neighbours and this can only be a good thing.

Last evening at 5pm, Jan and I were invited to drinks, courtesy of Zoom, by Gail and Tich, my sister- and brother-in-law in Bristol. Couples are even getting married on Zoom in this strange time. A risky business at best, as going online for your wedding runs the risk of bringing that girl you dumped in New Zealand out of the closet to shout from the back of the virtual church that she objects to the marriage.

I must admit that I was intrigued to see how this Zoom party worked out. In fact it works very well. The technology behaves perfectly and we all sit with glasses of wine and catch up on each others' lives. It is very relaxed, and one wonders if this is the new normal way of social intercourse. We are all great talkers, but try hard not to talk across each other. Normally, a conversation like this would have required a three-hour drive from Sussex to Bristol, a three-hour drive back home again, and a weekend of catering by our hosts. As Tich, a retired GP, is an inspired cook, that is no hardship for us. Zoom is not as good as being together under one roof. But it is great to see them and talk.

Our major shared concern is about when to leave lockdown, even when lockdown is lifted. Tich, I sense, is keen to get back to playing some golf. He says we should look at the Irish plan for easing lockdown, which seems to make a lot of sense. Both say that at present it looks like it will be September before we can think realistically of getting back to some kind of normality, seeing children and grandchildren and maybe having a meal out. Tich and Gail have been braver than us, ordering a pizza from an Italian restaurant around the corner which they collect themselves, wearing nitrile gloves. It was delicious, they say. Pizza: now suddenly the food of freedom.

We are only too aware that not everyone is eating pizza. Simon Tisdall, writing in *The Guardian*, says: "People in low-income and conflict-affected countries have so far largely escaped the high levels of Covid-19 infection seen in western Europe and the US, although this may be changing. The pandemic is killing them in different ways: lost jobs, ruined businesses, increased poverty, rising malnutrition and risk of famine, and a prospective increase in untreated, non-Covid preventable illnesses.

"For many of the most vulnerable, the developed

world's cures are proving worse than the disease. At the extreme, families must choose between going hungry and getting ill."

What a hellish choice this is.

Here in the UK, the focus is now on technology for the Track and Trace phone app to control the spread of the virus until we have a vaccine. But the Government's plan to exit lockdown through a tracking app will need detailed justification to satisfy human rights and data protection laws, a report has warned.

One can only imagine how this technology might be used by law enforcement agencies. It will be the end of our personal freedom and privacy. We will in effect be tagged and traceable each second of every day unless we leave our phones behind.

An NHS Track and Trace app aimed at limiting a second wave of Coronavirus will be trialled on the Isle of Wight this week.

It will be the first place where the new contact-tracing app will be used before being rolled out more widely this month, said Transport Secretary Grant Shapps.

The Government will be asking the whole of the UK to download it, he told the BBC's Andrew Marr Show. "That will help with a lot of the automation of the tracking."

Epidemiologists advising the NHS say that about 56 per cent of the UK population – equating to about 80 per cent of smartphone owners – need to use the app in order to suppress the virus.

And now, too, there is talk of health passports. Tech firms are in talks with Government ministers about creating health passports to help Britons return safely to work using Coronavirus testing and facial recognition.

Facial biometrics could be used to help provide a digital certificate – sometimes known as an immunity passport – proving which workers have had Covid-19, as a possible way of easing the impact on the economy and businesses from continuing physical distancing, even after current lockdown measures are eased.

The UK-based firm Onfido, which specialises in verifying people's identities using facial biometrics, has delivered detailed plans to the Government and is involved in a number of conversations about what could be rolled out across the country. This, too, has human rights implications.

Meanwhile at the pandemic coalface, in hospitals, doctors are wrestling with a condition known as 'Happy Hypoxia', a mystery condition which sees patients still breathing without much oxygen in their systems.

It is a mystery that has left doctors questioning the basic tenets of biology: Covid-19 patients who are talking and apparently not in distress, but who have oxygen levels low enough to typically cause unconsciousness or even death.

The phenomenon is raising questions about exactly how the virus attacks the lungs and whether there could be more effective ways of treating such patients.

A healthy person would be expected to have an oxygen saturation of at least 95 per cent. But doctors are reporting patients attending A&E with oxygen percentage levels in the 80s or 70s, with some drastic cases below 50 per cent.

It seems strange to be even thinking of lifting lockdown when we still understand so little about this terrible virus that is wreaking havoc across the world.

But running through my mind are the songs of the Jews and the Afrikaners, and the hope captured in the phrase *'Einde goed, alles goed'*. All's well that ends well.

This too will pass, this pandemic.

CHAPTER 29

4th May 2020

**Some people are pissed off, and some are just plain
pissed**

South Africans have had it tougher than us – no booze
or cigarette sales – and this is driving all the nicotine
and alcohol addicts crazy. You can't find a cigarette
butt on the streets of Cape Town and pineapples are not to
be had for love or money, as everyone is brewing their own
poteen or *witblits* (white lightning) at home.

There is all sorts of black-market stuff going on in
Cape Town, I hear from my contacts, as drinkers and smok-
ers are forced to be rather more creative than usual. I suspect
that every garden in the city is now growing cannabis to meet
the smoking demand, and that ginger beer has suddenly got
enough of a kick to give everyone the 'Malmesbury *brei*', the
guttural rolled R typical of real Afrikaners.

Cape Town supermarket shelves, already denuded of
loo roll, pasta and wheat flour, are suddenly short of yeast,
sugar and fruit too. And no pineapples!

President Ramaphosa may have saved thousands of
lives with his stringent lockdown, but Cape Town won't be
walking straight for a while, it seems.

A good friend, a doctor in Cape Town, known for

brewing his own beer, says he made a batch of ginger beer using pineapples and cane sugar a week ago and one evening had two glasses before supper 'to test it'. He was then called out from his home in Newlands to a patient in Seapoint, on the other side of the mountain. He said he only realised something was amiss when he could not find the road his patient lived in, and after a while, fuzzily realized he was in Llandudno, three miles further down the road – and fully three sheets to the wind.

He very sensibly called on his locum to take the Seapoint call and after a spine-chilling swim off the beach at Llandudno, drove home very slowly. Not an effect his normal homebrew or Pinotage had ever had on him, he said. I asked what had happened to the rest of the ginger beer, and he said he was saving it for a party when lockdown ended. It promises to be a party to remember.

Here too, we await our next delivery of food and drink with anticipation. Whole streets are now co-operating to keep each other topped up with essentials, and gossip and scandal are rife when someone asks for a mango on the WhatsApp group. A *mango*? My sister-in-law Gail tells me there was outrage on her street in Bristol when the request for this exotic fruit was made. Some people, it seems, do not realise that there is a kind of war on, as the politicians keep telling us. I just wish some of them would remember that after saving Britain from the Nazi threat (with a little help from our American and Russian friends – and men and women from every corner of Empire), Churchill, our war leader, was out on his ear at the first post-war election. Boris? You listening?

Our dog, Gus, is properly pissed off, as we've run out of tinned dog food and he is now on a diet of dog biscuits *du jour* and meat rinds from our plates. Not good enough it would appear, judging by his hangdog look. We may have rescued him from a dogs' home, but he did not sign on for such meagre rations, he seems to be saying. Our next Tesco slot will be heavy on dog food, if they will allow it. Thank God the cat, Saffy, is not currently moaning.

They don't realise how lucky they are. I tell them stories of WWII and the disappearance of pets into pots, but this falls on deaf ears; the last war is history as far as they are concerned, and their only concern is grub. Lots of it. Bit like us humans really.

And then disaster strikes. I have been jawing to Jan about Alec Hogg's introduction to the podcast of my book on BizNews, which mentions that Charles Dickens started the system of serialisation. Jan is much amused and gives me that old-fashioned look that says: "Don't get above yourself, mate." I don't see that it's that funny myself. Charles Dickens, after all, lived just up the road from us in Kent, and maybe, just maybe, I am channelling Dickens with my *Life in a Time of Plague*. But, jokes aside, you have to hand it to Alec, he takes hyperbole to a whole new level.

Suddenly the smoke alarm goes off, my toast and the toaster (which is on its last legs) are on fire in the kitchen. I've forgotten about it after jamming a wooden spoon handle in its side to hold the 'on' mechanism down, and coming upstairs to discuss my new role as the next Dickens with Jan. She says from now on my new nickname is not 'Dickens' but 'Big Dick!' And "Lucky the smoke alarm worked, or we would have had to jump out of the windows." Pride does indeed come before a fall. Luckily, the house is saved when I rush the toaster out to the garden, much to Gus's interest. Lockdown has its moments.

The UK Government has not yet published its plans for lifting lockdown, but cracks are appearing in lockdown anyway. One hears anecdotally of lockdown parties and today there are two confirmed, one in that great party town Liverpool, home of the Beatles. Police yesterday arrested 13 people and fined 11 others after raiding two Sunday lockdown parties in Liverpool. In a separate incident on Saturday, people travelled 20 miles from Manchester for a party in Wavertree. No doubt the trees were waving by party's end!

Twins were also stopped in Rochdale, Greater Manchester, on Saturday night after driving 17 miles to buy a kebab. As you do when the mood moves you, and only a kebab will do. Police impounded their car for 'serious vehicle defects'. The driver had no insurance, and the pair had travelled from Huddersfield, West Yorkshire, officers said. They don't mention whether the twins got to eat the kebabs. It would be good to know if the trip was worth it.

Looking at Ireland's five-stage lockdown exit plan, I realise just how complex this process in the UK is going to be, with no guarantees that it won't trigger a second wave of infection. This is a seat-of-the-pants operation, if ever there was one. And it will be the same the world over. The Irish Prime Minister, Leo Varadkar, has said that Ireland will begin the first of five phases in late May. Starting with small social gatherings and easing restrictions on funerals and outdoor activities, then progressing to allow more social and travel freedoms, come August the Irish will be able to go to pubs and small festivals again. So August will be one hell of a good time to be in Ireland. If you are not afraid.

One of the best overviews of how to get out of this catastrophe is summed up in *The Guardian* by Devi Sridhar, Professor & Chair of Global Public Health at the University of Edinburgh Medical School. He says that four months into the pandemic there are lessons we can learn about how best to control the virus and minimise deaths.

The first is to identify aggressively where the virus is and break chains of transmission using a 'test, trace, isolate' policy that involves mass community testing and putting all those testing positive into mandatory quarantine. The second is to protect health and social care workers who are most at risk. The third is to keep constant surveillance of the virus, using tracking systems to detect hotspots that are setting off more infection clusters. The fourth is to control borders. The fifth is to communicate honestly with the public to maintain trust and credibility in a sea of noise. The sixth is recognising that any 'exit' strategy is not like a switch and that means life will go back to pre-Covid-19 normal. A new normal will need to be adjusted to, which is likely to involve distancing, possible temperature checks in public buildings and offices and the use of face masks in public. The seventh lesson is that lockdown, if introduced early and quickly, can slow the spread of the virus. The final lesson is that all of the above are short term strategies while countries await the necessary scientific findings to make informed policy decisions and find the ultimate exit strategy.

Dr Sridhar concludes: "The steps above can ensure that countries keep daily new cases low and avoid a repeat of the 1918 flu epidemic which was determined, in the end, by the survival of the fittest."

That won't help me one little bit, that is for sure. The last time I might have been counted among the fittest would have been during my National Service in the Army in 1969. It's been all downhill since then.

CHAPTER 30

5th May 2020

Time travel

This pandemic has heralded a strange new fear – that of our fellow man, woman and child. It is not entirely a new fear, to be fair; we've been chary of each other for a long time. And not unreasonably. We've killed each other in war and at home, on holiday and at work, by day and by night, just about every and any chance we get in strange, bizarre and mundane ways. Just read the newspapers if you don't believe me. The greatest danger to humanity is humanity itself.

Any woman walking home alone at night is all too aware that any man poses grave dangers. Teenagers in inner cities fear other teenagers, gangs of us fear other gangs, and the elderly keep a wary eye out for everybody, young and old, who may simply push us over, deliberately or by mistake. Husbands kill wives at an astonishing rate, and now and again a wife will kill a husband. Sadly, it happens all too frequently. It is the people we know and who know us best who kill us; the statistics prove it.

We do not normally have to fear the whole of mankind, do we? But now we do, we have to. And it is a very strange feeling. Most of us are instinctively friendly, chatty and some of us like me, are quite touchy feely. I will reach out and touch a shoulder or an arm instinctively when chatting. Or take a hand. It is part of my Jewish and my Afrikaans heritage; *menslikheid* means humanity, an open-arms approach to life, to friends. And a lot of hugging. It is something I have had to try to wean myself away from, not always successfully, over the 40 years in England, which is more of a social distancing kind of place than a Latin hug, kiss and hug again kind of place.

But now this instinct to meet your fellow man more than halfway could kill you; literally, it could be the kiss of death, a Mafia-style hug that precipitates horror.

And it is so bloody hard. I find myself grabbing Jan by the back of her jacket, jersey or coat as she instinctively leans in, shortening the distance between herself and a friend or acquaintance as we walk up our lane, and we stop for a chat, or a car pulls up. She moves forward instinctively. "Pull me back when I do that, please," she has asked me, when she became aware of what she was doing.

It is difficult for her, as she is a massive communicator, a talker to rival me and has a big circle of friends. But, while I do like a chat to friends, Jan will speak to anyone, even total strangers. On trains, on buses, in shops, in restaurants, in public loos, on planes, in the street, Jan will reach out and make new friends. She makes friends everywhere, even as I and the kids pull back. "Oh God, here we go again," we think, she's chatting again.

I remember the young, good-looking firefighter from the US who had a window seat next to Jan on a flight from Heathrow to LA. He was heading home after teaching firefighters in Spain, something he did regularly, and was a 'smokejumper' – those crazy-brave firefighters who are dropped from helicopters into a blazing forest. They talked a blue streak that would have doused a thousand fires, the whole way. Jan had met her match! But now, now it is different. To talk like that could be death.

In some strange way, we are all time travelling. We've achieved a return to the 18th century, it is no longer 2020, it is once more 1720, with electricity and the internet, TV and radio, smartphones and laptops thrown in. But we have gone back in time, make no mistake about it. We do things like they did in 1720; we don't use planes or cars or buses if we possibly can. We stay home, we stay local, we stay put, we see almost nobody and we write endlessly to friends by email, just like Jane Austen and her contemporaries did when the Post Office provided a service that allowed for a same-day delivery of post across the land, such was the amount of letter writing going on.

We don't go out to shop: the grocer delivers. We may not send a servant or a child with a list to the shop, but instead we shop online and the delivery comes to us.

We make intimate contact with every nook and cranny in our homes and gardens, and lavish love and attention on our pets because we can't touch our grandkids or kids. We read voraciously, traveling vicariously, because that is what we have to do now, just as they did in 1720 when there were highwaymen lying in wait, cutthroats and pickpockets, disbanded soldiers with no work, roaming the land to rob and steal. Best to stay home with the door and windows barred at night. We are back there again. It might not last forever, please God that it does not, but for now we are living a kind of modern equivalent of 17th century life. And I quite like it. Aspects of it anyway. I'm not in any great rush to jump 300 years forward, back to 2020.

In some strange way that I don't understand, I have become a bit English in my 40 years living here. I no longer say: *"Kom maak 'n draai."* (Do pop in, come visit anytime). In fact, I'm a bit offended if people just pitch up at the front door, or I would be if they did, as it's England they don't, but you see what I mean. But now nobody knocks on your door. Even the postman or delivery drivers just dump your stuff and go. There are no distractions from the front door. And for a writer that is bliss incorporated. It makes me so happy. The drawbridge is truly, finally, completely up, and the moat is full!

And because few of us are working, the phones barely

ring, not much email either except junk, and there is quiet, hours and oceans of peace and quiet at last. It's going to be a shock going back to 2020 when all of this lifts. I am not going to like it, and I think that many other anti-social types would agree with me.

My late father would have hated lockdown; it was his habit to station himself outside our holiday house at the seaside resort of Bloubergstrand in the Cape, in the sure certainty that someone, a friend, acquaintance, a neighbor, would walk by and there'd be a chance of a chat. He was in seventh heaven one day when a German tourist coach disembarked its load at our front door – the house overlooked the sea which splashed up against the front retaining wall – and they all marched into the house and sat down to order tea and scones, thinking the place was a restaurant. Had my Dad had his way, he would have kept them there for lunch, afternoon tea and dinner. As it was, they just stayed for tea, embarrassed by their mistake but held there by my father's robust hospitality and desire to chat, to speak, to tell stories, to hold forth. This lockdown would have killed him.

It's hardly surprising that two of his children, my sister Jay and me, are still metaphorically speaking, hiding upstairs to avoid visitors. Our brother, Herman, on the other hand, is (metaphorically) in the road looking for tourist coaches. Aren't human nature and genetics strange?

The cottage still reeks of burnt toast and toaster, my daily reminder now that Charles Dickens and I only truly share one thing, a part of England that is home. But then he did not have the fun of podcasts, poor man. Eat your heart out, Charles!

Georgie, who has been looking after Callum for me, texted yesterday to say she had broken her foot. A horse stood on it; not Callum thank God. So now another friend, Alison who has helped us with our horses over the years, is going to take Callum on his daily walk down to pasture and back while Georgie in her plaster boot, will do the mucking out. We are lucky to have friends like this to help on the horse front.

A report just in changes my mood immediately. The

American publication Medpage reports that Covid-19 is killing African Americans at shocking rates. There are, it appears, wildly disproportionate mortality rates, and it highlights the need to address longstanding inequities. Infection rates are three times higher and death rates six times higher than among the white population.

In Louisiana, African Americans accounted for 70 per cent of Covid-19 deaths, while comprising 33 per cent of the population. In Michigan, they accounted for 14 per cent of the population and 40 per cent of deaths, and in Chicago, 56 per cent of deaths and 30 per cent of the population. In New York, black people are twice as likely to die from the Coronavirus.

Comorbidities like hypertension and diabetes, which are tied to Covid-19 complications, disproportionately affect the black community. But the alarming rates at which Covid-19 is killing black Americans extends beyond this, and can be attributed to decades of spatial segregation, inequitable access to testing and treatment, and withholding racial/ethnicity data from reports on virus outcomes.

"There is nothing different biologically about race. It is the condition of our lives," says Professor Camara Phyllis Jones, MD, former president of the American Public Health Association. "We have to acknowledge that now and always."

Many of these communities are located in poor areas with high housing density, limited access to education, and high unemployment rates. Low socioeconomic status is forcing some individuals residing in these communities out of their homes and into the workforce.

The Guardian's Rashad Robinson writes: "The failed and corrupt response to Covid-19 is killing black businesses, black jobs, black votes and black people. Deborah Gatewood was a black nurse who worked for 31 years in a Detroit hospital. Last weekend, she died from Covid-19 after being denied treatment by hospital doctors – four times.

"This fatal neglect may seem like a shocking individual story, but it is no surprise to those of us who have been tracking the many systemic inequalities in healthcare for years. As just one example, doctors routinely treat black people's pain and suffering far less seriously than that of other patients. It is the result of preposterous, anti-science assumptions they hold about black people, which their medical schools and hospitals still have not forced them to unlearn, as research studies have revealed."

He adds: "Even with factories shut down all across the country, one thing America never stops manufacturing is widespread racial injustice. Every day, we see how the unchecked racism that has pervaded our health system for years has become even deadlier now."

The story is much the same in the UK, where Black, Asian and minority ethnic people are dying in numbers out of all proportion to their presence in the population. The rich get richer and the poor get dead. Same old, same old. When will this ever change? If Prince Charles or Boris Johnson were black men, would they have survived Covid-19? You tell me.

CHAPTER 31
6th May 2020

Do I have the virus? I find myself understanding Trump.

I wake up at 6am as usual, and hear the impassioned singing of my mystery bird in the hedge next to my bedroom. His music comes through my window at high decibels and I have a light-bulb moment. I get out of bed, gingerly as ever, hold my laptop out the window on 'record', and capture 30 seconds of song. I will send it to my sister Jay and ask her to send it on to ornithologist Tim Dee, author of *Four Fields and Greenery* among others, to see if he can identify the canary-like trilling song for me. It would be so nice to know the name of this songster who lives cheek by jowl with me and whose song is better than any alarm clock.

The day feels like Sunday, and I have to think a bit to work out that it is in fact Wednesday. I remind myself that I have a Skype call booked for 9am with the University of the Free State in Bloemfontein, South Africa, a client of mine through Chapel & York. I wonder how they are managing in lockdown.

The 6am BBC news is led by an item on President Trump. He will shortly disband his Covid-19 Advisory Committee, even as deaths top 70,000 in the US, and replace it with an Economic Advisory Committee. He is signalling a political change of emphasis from trying to save lives to saving jobs. He says that he accepts that this policy will mean that he has to put out 'embers and even small fires' of Covid-19 infections, but that is what he will do.

Not for the first time in my life, I wonder if I have got it wrong politically with my liberal beliefs, and that Trump, for all his seeming craziness, is in fact, in this instance at least, crazy like a fox. In this life and death struggle that is in some ways like a game of chess, we have to accept the need to sacrifice pawns to save a Queen or King. Maybe America will be more accepting of a few thousand more deaths than the death of thousands of job-creating businesses and industries? I don't know, but I do know that the American voters knew what they were getting in Trump and voted for him anyway, and that he understands their mindset far better than I do.

The Jewish culture I grew up in believes that if you 'save one life you save the world', so for me the emphasis would always have to be life over money. But I also know that money means life to millions and its loss will mean death for too many. I would not make much of a general. I recognise that an effective warrior is prepared to sacrifice his soldiers to win a war.

I have been politically wrong so often in my life that I now distrust my own political judgement. I believed that the coming of democracy in South Africa in 1994 would be an unalloyed good and when it delivered Nelson Mandela, I felt vindicated in my beliefs, but then we got Jacob Zuma, who robbed the country blind and nobody touched him.

In Britain, during the Brexit campaign, I voted to Remain in the EU, assuming blithely that most British voters would agree with me, seeing economic and security self-interest as being the way to go, to remain part of one of the most powerful political forces for good in the world. I got that wrong, didn't I? It was close, but my side lost.

And America voted for Trump, although Hilary Clinton got the greater number of individual votes. My political antennae are suspect, and I no longer trust my own gut instinct on what people will do. So maybe, just maybe, Trump is right in this political judgment. Much as I despise him and all he stands for, I recognise that in the long run, in the greater scheme of things, he may be doing America a favour by sacrificing the lives of voters to fix the economy. Whereas, if I was President, I would beggar my neighbours by trying to save their lives.

But amid all the mayhem, there is suddenly, miraculously, very good news. I almost don't want to believe it. But it's all over the press: Reuters news agency breaks the story and everyone from *The New York Times*, to *The Jewish Chronicle*, to *The Times of India* is reporting it.

Israeli researchers have successfully completed the development phase of a Covid-19 antibody, in a significant step towards developing a viable vaccine for the virus. And if that is not good news, what is?

The findings at the Israeli Institute for Biological Research (IIBR) were announced in a statement by the Israeli Defence Ministry on Monday.

Israeli Defence Minister Naftali Bennett, who visited the Institute on Monday, said in statement that the step was a "significant breakthrough in finding an antidote for the Coronavirus".

He said: "I am proud of the Biological Institute staff, who have made a major breakthrough. Jewish creativity and ingenuity brought about this amazing development."

Mr Bennett's statement noted that the Institute was patenting the antibody formula and that an international manufacturer would be sought to mass-produce it.

Apparently, the antibody is derived from a single cell recovered from the blood of a patient who has recovered from Covid-19. These sources are seen as particularly promising in vaccine development. The Institute, which is based at Ness Ziona in central Israel, has been among the laboratories leading Israel's fight against Coronavirus.

A second Israeli research team at MigVax, an affiliate of MIGAL Galilee Research Institute, is also reportedly close to completing the first phase of development on a vaccine, and recently received an injection of $12 million to accelerate research.

Israel's Coronavirus picture has been gradually improving over the past few days. On Monday, the Israeli Health Ministry reported just 23 new cases of the virus over the previous 24 hours – the lowest daily rise in six weeks, while the number of patients on ventilators has also dropped to 76. Israel's death toll from the virus stands at 235.

Here in Britain, one of the scientific experts advising the Government on managing the virus, Professor Neil Ferguson, known as 'Professor Lockdown', has just resigned after breaking the rules to meet his married lover.

Professor Ferguson, the epidemiologist whose modelling helped shape Britain's Coronavirus lockdown strategy, has quit as a Government adviser after flouting the rules by receiving visits from his lover at his home.

Ferguson ran the group of scientists at Imperial College London, whose projections helped persuade ministers of the need to impose stringent physical distancing rules, or risk the NHS being overwhelmed.

In a statement on Tuesday, he said he was resigning his post on the Government's Scientific Advisory Group for Emergencies (SAGE), over an 'error of judgment'.

His lover, Antonia Staats, had crossed London from her family home to visit 'Professor Lockdown' on at least two occasions since the stay-at-home measures were imposed. Friends told the newspaper that Staats did not believe their actions to be hypocritical, because she considered the households to be one.

So, one rule for us and another for our masters. Same old, same old. I can only wonder if, after this excitement, the two households are still one.

In Prime Minister's Question Time at Westminster today Boris said: "I bitterly regret the care home epidemic." I bet he does, for all of the two seconds it took to say that. And he also said that from Monday May 11, the lockdown would start to be lifted. So Britain's time in lockdown is coming to an end. For how long nobody is sure; we may have to scurry back inside if a second wave of infection strikes. But one thing is certain, as we start coming out of our homes, we will be emerging into a world which is dramatically changed in many ways, and which will take years to fix.

Will we remember how we were let down at every level by this incompetent apology of a Government, or will we shrug it off and move on, complacent in the face of our unhappy dead and their grieving families, and our hurt and bewildered communities?

CHAPTER 32

7th May 2020

The joys of writing and podcasting in lockdown

My day starts each morning with the 6am BBC news on Radio 4, and as I lie in bed, I make notes of the headlines for expanding on later. This morning, it has emerged that the 400,000 surgical gowns from Turkey, that much vaunted delivery of protective clothing, do not meet British standards, are not up to the job, and will be sent back to Turkey ASAP. The PPE crisis, it seems, is still happening.

There has been a surge in bicycle sales, as many people fear to get onto buses, trains and tubes. So, perhaps, having killed so many of us, the virus will ultimately leave survivors a fitter bunch, and that can't be a bad thing.

The economic outlook is grim; the Bank of England forecasts a 14 per cent drop in GDP, the biggest for 300 years, but they say the economy will bounce back sooner than expected. Here's hoping.

Then a report that says many furloughed folk will find after lockdown that they don't have jobs to go back to. We are all flying blind, that is the truth of it. And I know just how dangerous that is. My mind goes back to 1971 in Cape Town when three Airforce 125 Mercurius jets flying in close formation, practising for part of the planned Republic Day celebration flypast, struck Table Mountain in thick fog, killing all three pilots and the other eight people on board.

Anyone who knows Cape Town is aware that its skies are dominated by that great, grey-blue looming colossus. Yet those pilots ploughed right into it and out of this world with a bang that echoed across the shocked city.

Yesterday afternoon, we decided to visit Robert and Jacqui Taylor's fabled bluebell field a mile from us. The night before, I had phoned to ask if this would be possible, and Robert had kindly said he would leave the gate to the field unlocked for us, so that we would not need to come to the house first. I parked my car by the gate, and we strolled through the small wood with its views beyond of the bluebell field and the heights of Ashdown Forest looming beyond in all its majestic palette of greens. As we emerged from the wood, the scent of the bluebells hit us in a wave, and we stopped, bewitched, filling our lungs with the intoxicating smell, and eating the blue and green views like so much eye candy. We agreed that we were blessed to live in this place.

We circled the field, photographing every possible angle, and then pulled up the two chairs at its edge to simply sit in the shade and observe the light-changing colours of the flowers, noting the odd patch of rare white bluebells among the sea of violet and purple blooms. We watched three horses, in their own green Eden beyond, meander in the warmth of the late afternoon sunshine.

Finally, we dragged ourselves away from this bliss, and walked back through the wood to the car. Just as we got there, Richard Wilkinson, our long-time horse guru and friend pulled up in his car. He was heading to his and Katherine Seymour's stable, where they run a professional horse-backing yard whose speciality is fixing problem horses. We stood well back from the car to talk.

Richard is a legend. He is the single most accomplished horseman I have ever known, utterly fearless and unfailingly kind to the animals that pass through his hands. He has saved the lives of countless horses that would otherwise have been put down. Often the problem is a skeletal issue that has led to such pain that the horse has become too dangerous to ride; or bad and inept human handling has created an angry, problem horse. Richard, now in his late 60s, with innumerable broken bones, a missing spleen, wrecked hips and crocked knees, keeps going, and gets onto horses I would never think of mounting. Many of them are, like Oscar Wilde, "mad, bad and dangerous to know", but he fixes them all, almost without exception.

I can remember some years ago, a huge black horse, almost 18 hands tall, whose favourite vice was rearing up with his rider and then throwing himself over backwards, determined at all costs to get rid of the man on his back and ideally pin him to the ground and kill him. He met his match in Richard.

Richard would exit left, throwing himself out sideways as the horse reached the pinnacle of its rear, and just before he fell over backwards. Once the horse had regained his feet, Richard would remount, and the deadly game would recommence. I am still not sure, even after knowing Richard for 35 years, if he is brave or mad. Probably a bit of both. He is a gentle, humorous man and yesterday teased me, saying he'd heard I was playing about with peas. A bit confused, I asked what he meant, and he said he believed I was making PODcasts. We laughed, and he drove on down to his waiting horses. Its just as well that he's a genius with horses, he's never going to make it as a stand-up comedian.

The audio recording of the book now takes up the start of each day. The sheer toe-curling horror of hearing the sound of your own voice takes some getting used to. A shot of Jameson's whiskey helped me through the first one. But a double whiskey at 10am is not a good idea, and things were a bit fuzzy till lunchtime.

In subsequent recordings, I can hear a tongue-licking sound at the end of each paragraph. Jan hears it too, and asks about it. I tell her the sound engineer in Jo'burg says it's not my tongue, but the opening and closing of my sphincter muscle. Jan has the best laugh I've heard from her in years when I tell her I've now disguised the sound with a second pair of underpants when recording. Tears flow as she laughs so hard it seems she might choke. It makes me happy to see her laugh like that.

The kind feedback I am getting is heartwarming. I hear from among others, old school classmates, and from former freedom fighter Marion Sparg, who was in our journalism class at Rhodes University, whose name will be inscribed in the history of South Africa, and who Jan featured in her book *Class of '79* about three anti-apartheid freedom fighters who studied with us there. And I hear too from Graham Watts, who in a unique way is father to these words, for though he is younger than me, it was he who taught me news writing at Rhodes, encouraged my life in journalism, and after he met up again with Jan when they both worked at the *Financial Times*, provided a platform for my work when he edited its weekend magazine. In his way he spawned a writing virus! Thank you Graham.

I fear the end of lockdown a little. The deep peace of this house arrest, and the hours of uninterrupted time it provides have become addictive. The ongoing conversations with family and friends round the world will be missed when work kicks in again, if it does.

One of the costs of emigration has been the loss of this daily contact with my sister and brother, with whom I am very close. The sibling bond has, if anything, got stronger over the years as I have always found them in my corner when the solids hit the fan. I value their wisdom and honesty and integrity and the fact that they put up with my teasing and joking. The loss of their company, their physical presence in my life, has been the single greatest cost of emigration. We joke that we are as close as we are because we each have a continent to ourselves: Africa, America and Europe. Thank God for them and my friends, who have made this strange time so productive and rich in so many ways.

Jan sends me a Twitter comment that delights me, as it will doubtless entertain many others who think Boris De Pfeffel Johnson is almost as bad as Covid-19. It is from Phil

Sparkes, and riffs off 'McCavity: The Mystery Cat' by T.S. Eliot:

De Pfeffel is a Mystery Man: he's known for his guffaw,
For he's the shady dilettante sidestepping the law.
He's playing wiff-waff in Beijing and being Churchill's heir,
But when the brown stuff hits the fan – de Pfeffel isn't there!

CHAPTER 33

8th May 2020

Boris's track record does not fit him well for any-thing

I wonder if I am missing something about the science be-hind the lifting of the lockdown. We have no vaccine, no magic bullet, so why are we even talking of letting people go out again freely? What about the warnings of a second wave of infection being worse than the first, as in the 1918 Flu Epidemic, which killed 50 million people?

Today the UK infection rate is at 12 per cent, so we need to be careful about any thought of an end of lockdown, says a scientist. We need to be ultra-cautious. If herd immuni-ty kicks in at 70 per cent, there will be a lot of illness and death to go through yet. We are a long, long, way from any light at the end of tunnel, as I see it.

I see a Twitter comment that sums up my feelings about this. It says: 'The end of stay-at-home orders doesn't mean the pandemic is over. It means they currently have room for you in ICU.'

But it is announced that from this Monday, May 11, rail services will resume, with up to 70 per cent of normal services running. What the hell?

Oliver Dowden, Secretary of State for Digital, Culture,

Media and Sport, speaking on BBC Radio 4 at the crack of dawn, says Boris's much-trumpeted speech on Sunday will announce 'small and tentative steps', not a blanket end to the stay-home message.

And if there is any indication of infection rising as a result, we will turn back to lockdown.

British police chiefs have warned that the lockdown is slowly ebbing away, with some warning that any further loosening will make key aspects of it 'unpoliceable'.

Several police chiefs told *The Guardian* that more people were going out by foot and road, and there were clear signs of people getting tired of lockdown. At least one force said it was scaling back part of its enforcement, for fear of losing public support.

The warnings come ahead of a long bank holiday weekend to mark VE Day, with the expected warm weather tempting people to go out after six weeks of restrictions.

West Yorkshire police assistant chief constable, Tim Kingsman, said: "At present, there has been no relaxation of the rules, so people shouldn't be thinking about large gatherings such as street parties."

Merseyside police said they would be stopping cars at random and that last weekend they had broken up several parties, with some people travelling from outside Merseyside to attend.

One chief constable in the South of England said his force expected to be busier than on New Year's Eve, with almost half the calls from the public 'snitching' on people allegedly breaching the lockdown.

There are other voices accusing the Government of giving mixed messages about the end of lockdown. The Welsh and Scottish governments are critical of the Government for ending the 'stay home' message. A major speech by Boris is being talked up for Sunday when he is going to speak about a 'road map to the end of lockdown'.

I fear that Boris's roadmap will look more like the driving of a drunk at the wheel, with violent swerves and drifting off at the curves. This is a man whose path to power is another zigzag roadmap which includes being fired from his job at *The Times* for fabricating two stories and for lying to Michael Howard, the Tory leader at the time, about his affair with Petronella Wyatt. In November 2004, Boris Johnson was a shadow arts minister under Howard, when it was reported in multiple tabloids that he had had a years-long affair with *The Spectator* columnist.

Boris publicly stated the allegations were untrue, calling them an 'inverted pyramid of piffle'. When proof of the allegations was presented, Howard asked Boris to resign, only for him to refuse, and therefore be fired for dishonesty for the second time in his career.

Then there was Boris's embarrassing time at the Foreign Office, and a personal life that sounds like comic opera, but which is closer to tragedy for those hurt by him.

With Boris at the wheel, God help Britain amid the corpses of more than 30,000 people, and as yet nobody is calling for his removal. And this is the man who is going to outline the roadmap ahead? Am I missing something here? I would like to get out of the car if Boris is at the wheel. When are the British people going to pull him over and remove him from the driver's seat?

Boris has been keen from the outset to paint the fight against coronavirus as a war. He should be very careful about this analogy, for when the dust has settled and the dead have been buried and we finally get back to some kind of 'normal', there is going to be a terrible reckoning to face, a forensic accounting, when this incompetent, insouciant, amateur Government undergoes a final analysis by historians and political thinkers for its performance during the pandemic. Boris may well be found to have been, in effect, utterly incompetent.

He did not prepare us for what was coming; he delayed and delayed, and gave the green light for mass gatherings including Cheltenham racing and Twickenham rugby; he had neither PPE nor ventilators in place; the huge NHS staff shortage (70,000 nurses alone) was the doing of his own and previous Tory Governments of which he was a minister; he allowed free movement in and out of our airports throughout this time. He was missing for five crucial COBRA crisis meetings when planning was underway to fight the fight to protect Britain. I don't think history will be kind to him.

It is the 75th anniversary of VE Day, the end of WWII in Europe, and the Government says celebrate at home with 1940s-themed tea parties. I get the sense that no one wishes to celebrate VE Day or anything else much. Maybe the very old who served in the armed forces would dearly love to, but they are locked up in total isolation in retirement homes. For those who sacrificed and are still alive, this second great public disruption of their lives must be a bitter pill, so close to the end.

It is a beautiful, sunny day and people are keen to go out and sunbathe on this lovely bank holiday weekend. That is all they really want to do: to lie in the sun and not think too much about the mess we find ourselves in.

But what of the lonely in lockdown? I wonder how the millions of people living on their own in Britain are coping? Loneliness in Britain is another plague, though it is an underreported one.

The number of people living alone has risen by a fifth over the last 20 years in what researchers deemed a 'statistically significant increase'. It rose from 6.8m in 1999 to 8.2m in 2019, with the majority of this increase driven by the growth in the numbers of men – predominantly aged between 45 and 64 – living alone.

Quoting rafts of research, The Campaign to End Loneliness reports: "Loneliness, living alone and poor social connections are as bad for your health as smoking 15 cigarettes a day. Loneliness is worse for you than obesity. Lonely people are more likely to suffer from dementia, heart disease and depression. Loneliness is likely to increase your risk of death by 29 per cent."

Half a million older people go at least five or six days a week without seeing or speaking to anyone at all. Over half (51 per cent) of all people aged 75 and over live alone, says the Office for National Statistics. Two-fifths of older people (about 3.9 million) say television is their main company.

I have known something of loneliness myself, and I know just how corrosive it can be. So, among the negative effects of the lockdown, the crisis of loneliness in Britain will not have been helped by it.

Doubtless there will be research in time that shows how the lonely coped during lockdown. Not well, I imagine. The economic cost of lockdown is plainly catastrophic for the country, but the long-term psychiatric costs to the population may be deeper and even more damaging in the long run. Time will tell.

For so many of us who are usually almost too busy to feel loneliness, this time of lockdown has brought an opportunity to reflect on our lives as no other time in the past decades. I hunt down a quote from a half-remembered poem that speaks best of this: *Leisure*, by William Henry Davies:

> *What is life if, full of care,*
> *We have no time to stand and stare?*

We have had weeks to stop and think, to stand and stare. What will this rumination bring to the life of the nation once we are back at work? Will it be just a bucolic dream, a national fantasy, or will some hard-edged change for the better come out of this time and space? To quote some management-speak, will we 'think out of the box', 'go back to the drawing board', or enjoy some 'blue sky thinking'?

I start my day, as ever, with coffee and toast, and after writing furiously, I record the next chapter of this book. Thank heavens for this project! It has been an absolute life saver and a joy. It has brought so many gifts, so many rewards, the sheer pleasure of writing about this weird time, learning the new discipline of podcasting, hearing from people who are hearing the podcasts or reading the book online, some of whom I have not heard from in 40 years or for longer; 50 years, in the case of an old friend with whom I used to ride as a teenager.

It is fascinating to hear about your life a lifetime ago as

seen by other people. In some strange way, they own a version of you that may be more real than that which you remember yourself. With my dodgy memory, that may well be the case!

From the living room, I hear the sound of Jan chanting her Buddhist daimoku, the way she starts each day without fail. It is a comforting sound, as I know she is chanting for my wellbeing, and that of her many friends and family. Buddhism for me feels like a step too far, having grown up with not one, but two religions, Judaism and Christianity: a third may strike God as sheer greed or indecisiveness. Who knows? For Jan, raised in the Church of England, Buddhism has become a mainstay of her life, and the end of lockdown when it comes, will bring with it a return to Buddhist meetings here at the cottage, instead of on Zoom.

For me, it will mean a return to my own church, the woods and green rides of Ashdown Forest.

Chapter 34
8th-9th May 2020

Hints that Britain will turn beggar

Last night, I made meatballs, or *frikadelle*, as they are known in South Africa. They were a huge success, if I say so myself. As someone who loves food and cooking, I have to admit that not all my dishes work out. And as this was a new recipe for me, one of my own making, I was particularly pleased. I served it with rice and a salad and a hot tomato & chilli sauce, which was the *pièce de résistance*. It made a good dish spectacular. And best of all, there was enough left over for lunch today.

As we are having lunch, I hear Boris's onetime boss at *The Telegraph*, Max Hastings, now a military historian, speaking about VE Day. He says what a poignant tragedy it was for those soldiers who died in the last days of WWII, when victory was assured, and for their families waiting for them at home with bated breath, counting the hours till they got home. How unspeakably cruel their deaths must have been for them and for their families, falling just before the finish line.

An image comes to mind of Wilfred Owen, the great WWI poet who died in its last week. On 11 November 1918, as news of the end of the war spread across the world, Owen's parents received notice that their son had been killed in action. The second lieutenant, who would become known as one of England's greatest war poets, had died while trying to lead his men across a canal at Ors, seven days earlier. He was one of thousands of servicemen killed in the last month of the war, and their deaths, coming as they did so close to the end of hostilities, have a particularly heart-breaking quality. His famous poem *Anthem for Doomed Youth* reads:

> *What passing-bells for these who die as cattle?*
> *Only the monstrous anger of the guns.*
> *Only the stuttering rifles' rapid rattle*
> *Can patter out their hasty orisons.*
> *No mockeries now for them; no prayers nor bells;*
> *Nor any voice of mourning save the choirs,—*
> *The shrill, demented choirs of wailing shells;*
> *And bugles calling for them from sad shires.*
>
> *What candles may be held to speed them all?*
> *Not in the hands of boys, but in their eyes*
> *Shall shine the holy glimmers of goodbyes.*
> *The pallor of girls' brows shall be their pall;*
> *Their flowers the tenderness of patient minds,*
> *And each slow dusk, a drawing-down of blinds.*

There is a lesson in this for us. Having survived the peak of the pandemic, let's not die now, when mopping-up operations are underway. Stay vigilant and stay safe; the war against Covid-19 is not yet anywhere near over, not until we've all been injected with a vaccine.

This VE Day is warm; it feels like the first true day of summer. I get hot walking back from my daily pilgrimage to Callum – 'He-who-shall-never-be-whipped-again!'

The owner of the bluebell field, our kindly roof-fixer and hedge cutter, Robert Taylor, has published a book of his poetry titled *A Lorry Driver's World,* which includes a poem called *Sixty Five Years On:*

> *Sixty five years on, the age a man can retire,*

> *Bullets shot, long ago, men under fire.*
> *Nothing remembered, lessons not learnt,*
> *And now poppies growing in ground that was burnt.*

I look up but see no victory Spitfires overhead on this peaceful bank holiday Friday, but far better in every way, there is indeed joy overhead. Our breeding pairs of swallows are knitting the air between the cottage and the stables, with swooping dives. Pearl and plain, pearl and plain, their clicking sounds fill the air.

I am full of lunchtime *frikadelle*, and pretty damn good they were too. I can hear Jan and the kids in years past, teasing me at suppertime by echoing my claim, "Well this is *delicious*, if I say so *myself*", words I always use, they say, when I am appreciating the genius of my own cooking.

And speaking of food, things don't look so good for any future post-Brexit trade deal with the US, now that we are leaving our major trading partner, the EU. *The Independent's* political sketch writer Tom Peck reminds us that President Obama warned that if Britain voted for Brexit, it would go "to the back of the queue" for a trade deal with the US. Britain ignored that advice, and its role is now that of a tramp, says Peck, waiting hopefully at closing time, by the bins, out the back of America.

Peck says rumours have emerged that US trade officials have been referring to the forthcoming trade deal as the United States United Kingdom Agreement, USUKA for short, pronounced 'you sucker'. Such rumours may not be true. But the truth within is self-evident.

So even after lockdown ends, there will be more mountains to climb for a newly impoverished Britain, begging at America's door.

News from the White House indicates they have their own problems much closer to home. Two personal aides to President Trump and Vice President Pence have tested positive for Covid-19, and a number of staffers were taken off the President's plane to be tested, as he prepared for a trip to Camp David.

There is a huge, full, looming 'Super Moon' hanging in the sky these last two nights, whose silver beauty catches at the throat. The sight reminds me of the wonderfully named Kirsty Moon, a professional horsewoman who helps me with Callum when I have to be in London or abroad for work. She has posted a poem on social media that casts a cold lunar light on this time we are struggling through, and it is no surprise that young people are despairing. Here is a taste.

"...Warnings rang out amongst us, but humanity proved too strong willed. Woods became concrete jungles and manmade scars were etched upon the Earth. We lost sight of nature's beauty. Of the simplest things and their greater worth. A land, that with less human presence, began to heal the wounds of our relentless abuse. It became clear – that to Earth humans were the virus – and for this there should be no excuse. We must learn to treat the world as our ally – for we need it more than it needs us."

The radio news today reports that when Britain reopens for business, any travellers returning to the country will have to self-isolate for 14 days, which will put paid to most people having a summer holiday. People arriving in the UK from any country apart from the Republic of Ireland will be asked to quarantine themselves for a fortnight: that's according to UK airlines, who say the Government will introduce the restriction from the end of this month in response to the Coronavirus outbreak.

And the over-70s will be advised shortly to stay in lockdown until June. On Sunday, the Government is expected to announce how lockdown rules will start to be eased, and there has been speculation that the over-70s might be treated differently to the rest of the population. There are about nine million people over 70 in the UK, which is about 14 per cent of the population. The Office of National Statistics figures up to April 2, show that 81.5 per cent of the deaths in England and Wales, where the virus was mentioned on the death certificate, were for people aged over 70.

Our love of gardens in Britain is one of our best characteristics. Now it seems that visiting gardens will also become something we do online. A friend, George Plumptre, the CEO of the National Garden Scheme, has announced this new measure. Every year about 3,500 gardens open to visitors for the NGS, but this year the organisation expects its income to be down by 80 per cent. For 90 years, the National Garden Scheme has given people the chance to visit some of the best private gardens in England and Wales and has given more than £60m to health charities, raised through admission charges as well as the sale of tea and cakes.

But Coronavirus has forced these thousands of gardens to close to visitors for the first time in the scheme's long history. This year, gardeners will be showing off their efforts with videos, while urging people to donate money online as they meander virtually around the flowerbeds and lawns. Gardener and TV presenter Alan Titchmarsh has shared a tour of his garden near Alton in Hampshire, filmed last year, to encourage others to participate and donate. He said: "Our gardens offer us a sheet anchor in times of turmoil – never more so than this year."

Jan and I feel blessed to have a garden to ourselves. It has been our retreat during this time of lockdown. We have felt less cut off, thanks to our time in its green spaces, watching the plants we have filled it with over four decades come to bloom this spring. Each day that the weather is good we both write. Jan is finishing a new novel. Her previous three books were well received: Her most recent, *The World Beneath*, a young adult novel set in the apartheid era in South Africa, won a literary award in the US for its American edition, and was endorsed by Amnesty International 'as contributing to a better understanding of human rights and the values that underpin them.'

This old cottage will soon have seen eight books emerge from it over the years, as well as countless articles, journalism and features. It is a rural word factory. I look up some words I wrote in 2006, as Jan and I sat working in the garden.

Cloud Comets

Silver-tipped cloud-comets cross the sky to and from Gatwick,
Lending added peace to the garden
As I sit, this perfect summer evening.
A pregnant cat crosses the lawn in search of sanctuary.
Crows argue and sheep bleat their dusk note.
Swallows harvest the near air,
As I contemplate my life.
Above, the cargoes of hope and despair
Trail plumes of sex and death and laughter
Like my own life, my own trail.
And beside me, my love, you sit, still there
After all these years.
A bright star in parallel orbit, trailing cares and kids and joys.

Dotty Britain is alive and well. British diplomats around the world will be running online to raise money for charity today. These are the much-criticised folk who were responsible for the repatriation of one million Brits from abroad, and now they are on the run.

British Government staff in diplomatic posts around the world will take part in a live, 24-hour global relay marathon to raise money for charities on the frontline, battling Covid-19. From Samoa to Vancouver, the 'Diplomile' will cover 101 countries over 23 time zones, travelling from East to West.

At the same time, it's reported that thieves and con-men across Britain are cashing in on Coronavirus panic, selling fake facemasks and gloves among other scams. More than 500,000 unusable facemasks, and a garage selling fake Covid-19 testing kits, are among the hundreds of frauds investigated by trading standards officers since the start of the lockdown.

You've got to love Britain! A panic brings out the best in us, and the worst. But the gung-ho buccaneering spirit is alive and well.

CHAPTER 35

10th May 2020

Dying at home for fear of hospitals

Today is going to be the warmest of the year thus far, with temperatures peaking at around 25 degrees. I have breakfast in the garden, and it is already warm at 9.30am, with the promise of a beautiful day ahead.

The Columbine fairy flowers (Aquilegia) that we've planted in the bed behind the kitchen are at their best in blues, mauves, white and violet, and have self-seeded into the grassed-over path up the garden. You never know what new and unusual colour they will come up with.

I'm glad I have not mown the horse-path up the side of the garden this year, otherwise I'd not have known about this lovely spread of the Columbines. They are doing well in this area, as it is the most protected from the scything winds we get up here on this hill from time to time as they sweep in off the Atlantic in south westerly blows or in winter north easterlies off the Russian Urals, a blast that chills you to the bone.

Because it is going to be such a warm day, we decide to give my car a run to keep the battery charged and go and visit Traveller, Jan's horse, at livery about five miles away. We find him alone in the huge 20-acre field, swathed in his light-weight fly rug and mask, looking for all the world like a

Tudor charger ready for a joust. He ambles over to enjoy the apple Jan has brought for him, mouthing it awkwardly and dropping it on the ground, before picking it up to finish it off with relish.

At the stables we find Deborah and her daughter Abbey and some of her clients, Peter, Claire and Heather, who are just back from a ride. They say they passed three other riders, and that the Forest is being used much as usual by walkers and riders. We've had Traveller at this lovely yard run by Deborah for three very happy years now. She is wonderful with the horses and the clients too. In our three years there she has spotted a number of eye and other issues that Traveller has had and has nursed him back to health.

We take Gus for a mile-long walk across the estate to the gate and into the Forest proper, a stroll that passes magnificent trees and offers far-ranging views out onto Ashdown Forest, and in the hazy distance, the hump-backed South Downs. A gracile, black dog joins us for the walk. She has huge bat-ears and looks like the dogs one sees in ancient Egyptian tombs. She is friendly, and wants to play with Gus, who rather huffily ignores her and trots on, taking his own line.

Back home, I rustle up some lunch of leftover sausage, diced into mushrooms fried in butter with some crisped cauliflower. We sit in the garden under the Chinese dogwood and enjoy the meal. Afterwards, a bit dozy with the heat, I do something I've not done for a long while, head off inside for an afternoon nap. Normally on a Saturday afternoon I would watch racing, but racing has been cancelled for weeks now as has all sport. I fall asleep at 2.30pm and wake at 4.15pm feeling refreshed. Jan brings me a cup of tea in the garden.

Later, as the day cools, I grab a beer and grill a small spatchcocked chicken and we eat in the garden again, three outdoor meals in one day, not bad going for England. After supper, we take Gus for a walk up the lane.

When we get back home, we watch a documentary about Michelle Obama's 34-stop book tour of America, to promote her autobiography, titled *Becoming*. She is a truly remarkable human being, intelligent, charming, witty, funny, self-deprecating, grounded, and wise. We are filled once more with admiration and respect for her. She absolutely exemplifies grace, and if it is possible, embellishes that quality. Obama was a lucky man to find her. It is evident that she is a strong, independent woman and talented lawyer who bears the scars of her upbringing in Chicago and those inflicted on the campaign trail for her husband. She and her story are remarkable, and the power of her smile could light a small city. Surrounded as we are these days by evil pygmy politicians, we can only count our luck to have lived in a time that has produced Nelson Mandela and Barack Obama, and this woman who has every qualification to make a truly great President herself.

By happy co-incidence, I'm reading *The Warmth of Other Suns*, by Isabel Wilkerson, a winner of the Pulitzer Prize. It is the epic story of America's great black migration from the south to the north to escape the violence and poverty of the plantation life. This Christmas gift book is from Steph, our son Dominic's partner. The book chronicles the journey north by millions of black people, a trail that Michelle's family themselves took. She points out that her great-grandfather was a slave. Four generations from slavery to the White House – now that is a story and a heritage to amaze anyone.

The news today has been something of a downer, focusing as it does on the collateral damage of the Covid-19 virus. *The Guardian* reports that about 8,000 more people have died in their own homes since the start of the Coronavirus pandemic than in normal times. Concerns are growing over the number of people who are avoiding going to hospital.

Of that figure of 8,000, 80 per cent died of conditions unrelated to Covid-19, according to their death certificates. Doctors' leaders have warned that fears and lessened priority for non-Coronavirus patients are taking a deadly toll.

Some sick people are just too scared to go to hospital and are aware that much of the usual NHS care has been suspended in the pandemic. "These figures underline that the devastation wrought by Covid-19 spreads far beyond the immediate effects of the illness itself," says Dr Chaand Nagpaul, the council chair of the British Medical Association.

"While all parts of the NHS have rallied round in a bid to meet the immediate rocketing demand caused by the pandemic, more than half of doctors in a recent BMA survey have told us that this is worsening the care of non-Covid patients."

He cites a fall in A&E visits of up to 50 per cent and a drop by half of patients attending hospitals with heart attacks.

"Referrals from GPs are not being accepted unless for serious medical conditions, and routine investigations to aid diagnosis are not available in many cases. This means many ill patients are not getting the care they so desperately need now – and crucially, risking their conditions getting worse, and with some even dying as a result," Nagpaul adds.

Prof Andrew Goddard, President of the Royal College of Physicians, says excess community deaths from non-Covid causes had been seen across Europe. A report this week found that there had been about 11,600 such fatalities in Italy during its pandemic, including deaths from heart attacks and strokes.

"Data from other countries has shown delayed presentation in patients with heart attacks during the pandemic, either because people don't want to burden the health service at the current time, or because of fear of catching Covid-19. It is critical that patients who are worried they may be having a heart attack or stroke should call 999."

Jan and I are only too aware of this issue. She has been nursing a cracked rib, and I keep a close eye on my various medical problems. If either of us needed medical attention right now we know we would be risking the virus if we went anywhere near a medical facility and would then run the risk of infecting each other. It is a low level, but constant concern.

But tomorrow, something to really look forward to: Boris will broadcast his 'roadmap' out of this slow-evolving Coronavirus car crash that he drove us into. It will be less amusing than the Goon Show. Peter Sellers, Harry Secombe, Spike Milligan, where are you now that we need you so badly? We told you we were sick!

I take refuge from the current madness as I do so often, by going riding in my head. On one of my last rides just before lockdown, I met someone special in the woods.

It was 7pm and there was the slightest breeze up on the open forest, so I put Callum into a slow rolling canter to the top. And from there it was back down into the woods above our cottage. We stopped as usual to admire the three pigs that Maurice and Julie are raising on their smallholding along with the three red chestnut Sussex steers – all destined for their deep-freeze. Callum is happy to stand there endlessly, even though he knows we are now on the home run. He's a bit of a dreamer this horse, not unlike the man on his back.

And then, as we moved off, I saw a movement in the tree shadowed path ahead, a small, rather ancient, flea-bitten fox stopped to look over his shoulder at us. Callum spotted him too and lifted his head to peer at him hard, got his scent and walked briskly to catch up. We closed in on the fox who was totally unfazed. He trotted left off the path, up the earth bank into the woods, stopping to peer at us from behind an oak, looking like something out of a children's book.

I said: "Good evening!" Ignoring me, the fox turned and walked another twenty feet into the wood and then like an old dog lay down and curled up at his ease on some leaf mould, a 'Prince of the Wood' at his leisure.

It struck me that the three of us were not that different – fox, horse and man – we all love these owl-haunted woods and know their paths and secret byways. This is home, after all, and all the more precious in lockdown.

CHAPTER 36

11th May 2020

Boris only speaks for England

There is a cool wind blowing from the west this morning, rocking the branches of the huge neighbouring oak tree and the poplar, lower down the valley, but the sun is shining intermittently.

The much-vaunted Prime Ministerial broadcast last night was vintage Boris. The speech about lifting lockdown was as clear as mud. His address to the nation was immediately condemned as divisive, confusing and vague, and the leaders of Scotland, Wales and Northern Ireland all said they would not be changing the 'Stay at Home' message to his new 'Stay Alert' message, which signified nothing.

The country was on red alert, even before Boris woke up to the dangers posed to Britain by the pandemic, (bragging as he did of shaking hands with Covid-19 patients) and omitting to mention that he had missed five emergency COBRA meetings. We all had a fair idea what was coming, if you exclude the 250,000 steeplechase fans at Cheltenham who took a racing bet on their chances of living or dying (at what odds I wonder) and the 80,000 rugby fans at the Six Nations game. I hope none of them found themselves scrumming with Covid-19, but I suspect many did.

The Labour Party today is immediately critical, saying workers need to know that they will be safe if they go to work, as the PM has suggested. At the same time, the PM said please avoid using public transport; instead, use the car, cycle or walk. It was, at best, confusing, and no use at all for those who need to go to work by train.

Speaking from Downing Street, Boris looked healthy and rather more spruced up than usual. Someone had brushed his hair, and he was even wearing a tie. He said that if the circumstances were right, schools in England and some shops might be able to open next month, and the Government was 'actively encouraging' people to return to work if they cannot work from home.

But he stressed that this was "not the time simply to end the lockdown", and that he intended to take a cautious approach, guided by science, otherwise a second deadly wave of the 'devilish' virus would take hold.

'Stay at home, protect the NHS and save lives' - used since the beginning of the outbreak in the UK - has been ditched and replaced with 'Stay alert, control the virus, and save lives.'

His remarks drew criticism and concern from across the political spectrum – and his decision to drop the 'Stay at Home' message in favour of the vague advice to 'Stay Alert' was met with howls of rage and bitter humour on social media. The new 'Stay Alert' message has been ruthlessly mocked, with Brits coming up with their own satirical versions.

Some of my favourites include:

"Ooh careful, mind how you go. Stay lucky."
"Sneak up, shout at the virus, then run."
"Do as you please, we're not fussed if some of you die."
"We haven't got a fucking clue what we are doing."
And finally:
"I'm staying home thanks."

The last one echoes my own thoughts on this.

Though he gave no details, Boris described his blueprint for a gradual easing of the Coronavirus lockdown in England, which could see primary schools, shops and nurseries partially open from June 1, and some cafes and restaurants with outdoor space too. Places of worship, and cinemas with socially distanced audiences, could open for business from July.

He was mocked from the left and right of the political spectrum for his message, which essentially said you could go to work unless you couldn't, and that now you could get as much exercise outside as you wished as long as you maintained social distancing, and if you misbehaved, fines would be much bigger now. And if the infection started to rise again, he would put the brake on hard and go back to square one. The speech just served to confuse a confused nation further.

There is a shopping basket of baffling stories in the media this morning.

A *Sun* and *Sunday Times* survey reveals that 90 per cent of Britons don't want the lockdown lifted and are happy to stay home for longer if needed.

Teachers have asked: how do you keep children in primary school safe? How do you keep the toys for the little ones Covid free?

London Mayor Sadiq Kahn says he is not lifting the lockdown in London. He says people should avoid using public transport if they have to go to work. And if you can't maintain social distancing, stay home. "As I speak to you, people are dying in London. If we lift the lockdown, we risk a greater second peak." He said 29 London bus drivers had died so far.

Specsavers are speaking of Zoom based eye testing, but I just can't see it working.

Travellers from France will not be tested at British airports or required to go into 14 days of self-isolation.

On the Isle of Wight, a 'track and trace' app trial is launched today, with a good pick-up by people on the island, it is reported. If it is shown to work, the whole of Britain will be asked to join, so that we can track the spread of Covid, and maybe monitor Cabinet ministers meeting their mistresses.

And the BBC reports that sex workers are still active and travelling the country to meet clients at their homes. They need to feed their families, they have told reporters.

I help Jan's sister Gail to get a press release out for her employer, the mental health charity The Bridge Foundation. It is warning that there will be long term damage to family life in Britain, because of mental health issues during lockdown, and is offering support through Zoom and other social media mechanisms.

The release states: "The Bridge Foundation therapists support people of all ages with a huge range of issues such as anxiety, depression, self-harm, gender identity or sexuality, trauma, bereavement and family breakdown, or relationship difficulties.

"During this current pandemic, there are many additional reasons why families and individuals of all ages are coming under pressure. For some, existing anxieties and phobias are increased; for some, child (and adult) behaviour becomes more challenging as people experience more frustration, or as anxiety tips into anger; others might find themselves retreating into themselves and feeling higher levels of despair and hopelessness, struggles with sleep or difficulty concentrating.

"The team of therapists at The Bridge Foundation have adapted the therapy and counselling they provide for online and phone appointments. They are finding that through the use of technology, it's possible to support families effectively. This includes supporting parents to better help their children, helping with family dynamics and working with individual children and young people directly, as well as providing therapy for adults."

Throughout the day, the tennis match between Boris supporters and his opponents hits the issue of 'Stay Alert' instead of 'Stay Home' backwards and forwards across the airways.

So here in the UK this week, we wait some more; wait to see more detail of Boris's and Dominic Cummings's plans for us, and keep a watching brief on the voices from Scotland, Wales and Northern Ireland, from the media and the Labour Party, as we try to finesse the odds of how we will deal with reintegration into society. I recall the prediction that by the time all this madness ends, 80 per cent of us will have caught it. Not great odds for someone my age, so lockdown seems to be the only way, to just sit it out for as long as I can, and hope and pray that a vaccine is created soon.

CHAPTER 37

12th May 2020

Spending is 40 per cent down as we stay home waiting

The day starts icy, with frost silvering the lawns and fields. The temperature at 6am is 2 degrees Celsius. It is a much colder start to the week, with some Arctic air across the UK this morning.

Boris and his ministers are sending out a message following the 'roadmap' crash. "Use your common sense about going to work, going outside, using public transport." This is a bit rich coming from a Government which would do well to find some common sense itself. And not much clearer than the original.

I feel fat, unfit, and tired, which is both understandable and ridiculous, given the amount of sitting and lying around I'm currently doing. This is a common reality I suspect, as many of us have fallen victim to some strange kind of 'holiday' syndrome. There has been no need to get up for work for the past six weeks for those of us who are not frontline workers, so we lie late in bed, every day a Sunday morning, minus the comforting sounds of BBC Radio 2's *Steve Wright's Sunday Love Songs*. And we go to bed later and later.

For those of us furloughed or on 80 per cent of salaries,

there is the added pleasure of this being a kind of paid holiday, although we know the flight back to work may be bumpy, and once we arrive, there may well be no job. We've all become news junkies. We lie around, eat too much and stay up late, to midnight and beyond, watching film after film, video after video. It's not great for our physical or mental health. It feels less like a war and more like imprisonment, or a very boring holiday. Instead of fighting, we are waiting, just waiting.

There is one benefit - our spending is down by 40 per cent. A recent study of our bank account activity shows that we are keeping what money we have in the bank. We are not spending nearly as much on buying coffees, doughnuts, sandwiches or pies, we are not making impulse buys at the supermarket or anywhere else, we are not using petrol or diesel, we are not booking holidays. This is all true of me and many millions, I'm sure. Our main spend is on food and that's it. We wait. Trying to foster common sense.

There is a small local good news story. A man who went missing for two days from his home in Kent, suspected of being on Ashdown Forest, has been found. The father-of-three went missing on Thursday but has been found safe and well, police have confirmed. He was found by rescue teams on Ashdown Forest on Sunday. He had last been seen driving to the Forest last Thursday, but as he had no mobile phone on him, his family became increasingly worried. The search was heavily focused on the Forest, with specialist rescue teams searching the area. The police searched down our lane and in the woods. Riders kept a sharp lookout for him too. There is general relief that he has been found.

Over the years, there have been a number of suicides found in these woods. Strange how often, like the animals we are, we crawl into the depths of nature, into deep brush or wood to die. Happily, on this occasion, the lost man was found. I believe some 600 people were involved in the search. I am glad to know he is once more at home with his family.

There is also a small, fragile symbol of hope growing around the back door of the cottage. The self-seeding Col-

during his National Service, he was told to fall in at some God-forsaken hour of the morning, which he did, but as a protest he emerged in his helmet, boots, webbing and nothing else, naked as the day he was born. If you decide to use the 'cannabis spliff' image of me (which I heartily encourage), I would request one of Guy in said battle undress."

And so my day is immeasurably lightened with laughter and humour. It is not lost on me that tonight is the 15th anniversary of Guy and Jay's son Kirsten's death 15 years ago. The fact that they are both able to live their lives with humour and laughter after such agony and its unhealed wound is the greatest indicator of their mental strength and wellbeing, and a testament to their marriage.

All of this is a timely reminder to me not to let the lockdown get me down, and to lighten the load of waiting. Others close to me have been through something so much worse and emerged full of the joys of life. I can wait a little longer.

Chapter 38

12th May 2020

The virus is here to stay

The official death toll in the UK from Covid-19 today stands at 40,496, according to official figures (with almost 10,000 care home residents now having died from Covid-19). The total figure is closer to 50,000, according to a variety of organisations analysing the death count. And the Government's message is 'Stay Alert'. Oh, that Boris and his chums had 'Stayed Alert' when they held the lives of the 50,000 dead in their hands three months ago.

Eight million people with underlying health conditions should be exempted from plans to get the country back to work and normal life, according to scientists who warn that easing lockdown too quickly could propel the Covid-19 death toll to 73,000 this year. About 80 per cent of the population have little to fear from a return to work, but 20 per cent are vulnerable because they have one or more common conditions such as diabetes, obesity and heart problems, say researchers from University College London (UCL) in a *Lancet* study published on Wednesday.

Once in a while, I hear a voice on the radio, usually a scientist, never a politician, who makes sense of it all, who gives real brutal truths. This lunchtime on BBC Radio 4, I heard a scientist, Dr John Lee, a retired professor of patholo-gy, say: "Bottom line is, we are going to have to live with Covid-19." He said nothing was as yet entirely clear about what was happening with the virus, nor if our lockdown was affecting the virus's behaviour, inhibiting its spread or the way it might mutate.

Dr Lee said: "Results from many countries with more or less stringent lockdowns are showing much the same sort of results. The 'R' issue is so beset with statistical issues that it is not reliable. Sweden's approach may prove in the long run to have been the most sensible. All epidemiology modelling for the behaviour of the pandemic is more akin to weather fore-casting than laboratory science, and we know how often the weather forecasters get that wrong. We have to ask ourselves, would we be willing to suffer this kind of dramatic change to our lives based on long-term weather forecasting? Because that is essentially what we are doing with this virus."

Currently, scientists are saying that just 5 per cent of the population have been infected with the virus and to achieve 'herd immunity' that figure needs to be close to 70 per cent. This is going to be a very long haul. Governments are casting around for a way to map us out of lockdown and some, like the UK government, have settled on the 'R' num-ber as the way to go. But because it is based on changing variables, like how infectious the disease is, its value is limited.

Dr Lee adds: "What the lockdown has done is to flat-ten the curve of the initial spike and help the NHS to build up extra capacity. Unless we turn ourselves into a North Korea, and keep the population locked down forever, the virus is going to spread again. What we should be doing, like Swe-den, is finding a sustainable way to live with this virus. We should not go into panic mode and stay stuck indoors waiting for the sky to fall on our heads, only coming out when we think it has passed, only then for the virus to start spreading again. We have certainly bought ourselves some time by lockdown in which we have a better prepared NHS, a better understanding of the virus and supportive treatments. But we are going to have to learn to live with the virus."

So, as I listen, I understand one thing, we see through a glass darkly, we don't understand much, we are blind, and we are fumbling our way gingerly out of a pitch-black room into a new world in which lurks the Coronavirus crocodile. God help us all. And Boris is at the helm.

Rishi Sunak, the Chancellor, is getting to seem like the good guy in all this mayhem. The UK scheme to pay wages of workers on leave because of Coronavirus will be extended to October, he has said; the Government backed workers and companies going into the lockdown, and would support them coming out. Mr Sunak confirmed that employees will continue to receive 80 per cent of their monthly wages up to £2,500. But he said the Government will ask companies to "start sharing" the cost of the scheme from August. Some 7.5 million workers are now covered by the scheme, up from 6.3 million last week.

Mr Sunak said: "I'm extending the scheme, because I won't give up on the people who rely on it. Our message today is simple: we stood behind Britain's workers and businesses as we came into this crisis, and we will stand behind them as we come through the other side." He also rejected suggestions that some people might get 'addicted' to furlough if it was extended. "Nobody who is on the furlough scheme wants to be on this scheme," the Chancellor said. "People up and down this country believe in the dignity of their work, going to work, providing for their families. It's not their fault their business has been asked to close or they have been asked to stay at home."

There are new rules under the 'Stay Alert' flag: People in England are allowed to spend more time outdoors: for example, to have a picnic in the park, provided they observe social distancing. They can also exercise as much as they wish and play certain non-contact sports like golf, tennis or basketball with one other person from outside their household. However, they are still unable to use areas like playgrounds and outdoor gyms, where there is a higher risk of close contact and touching surfaces. People in England are free to drive as far as they like to outdoor open spaces. But they should not travel to Wales, Scotland or Northern Ireland, or stay anywhere else overnight, including at a second home.

I spend the whole day outside writing in the garden, writing this book, and also doing work for clients. After supper, Jan has a Zoom meeting with local Buddhists. I watch TV for a while, *Ray Donovan* again. At 9pm I go outside and walk up the lane in the dark and say a quiet prayer for Kirsten, my lost nephew whose anniversary this is, and for his parents.

We are surrounded by the statistics of the dead: what is one life in the midst of all of this? But our experience of Kirsten's death and the pain of his loss fills the number 'One' to bursting point, so I have some idea how 40,000 to 50,000 families are feeling tonight. Their loved ones may add to the statistics, but for them he or she meant the world and they will be experiencing the agony of disbelief, of waiting for the front door to open, and to once more see the beloved face come in. Each time the door opens, they will look up to see if it is not the lost one returned. That is how it is.

The pandemic is delivering death on an industrial scale. Covid-19 is factory-farming humans; it is a cull in human flesh. Imagine the piles of dead, the equivalent size of the population of three small towns. And yet I don't hear a sound, there are no mobs on our streets screaming blue bloody murder. There is just grief and fear and disbelief that this tectonic change to our lives can be happening. I can only wonder once more if some form of retribution will be measured out to those who swore to protect us as they took the reins of Government?

I won't be surprised if no politician is brought to book. Look at what happened in 2008, when bankers destroyed the international economy which led to ten years of impoverishment for millions. Did you see one banker jailed? There were no guillotines in Trafalgar Square, no firing squads in Piccadilly, we just suffered under the Government rule known as 'Austerity' for ten years – which itself killed many people – and we got on with it. There was no magic money tree we were told. Now a forest of magic money trees has been found.

What will it take to rouse this country? What will England say, when England finally speaks?

Chapter 39

13th May 2020

Dancing with the Devil

As of today, May 13, (lucky for some) people in England can spend more time outside, meet a friend at the park and move home, as the Government begins easing some lockdown measures. And the day delivers some insights into what our future will look like.

Under the new rules, garden centres can reopen, and people can meet one person from outside their household. Sports that are physically distanced – such as golf and tennis – are also now permitted. And some employees who cannot work from home are being encouraged to return to their workplaces.

This follows the speech by Prime Minister Boris Johnson on Sunday in which he unveiled a 'conditional plan' aimed at reopening society, much of which has been in lockdown for seven weeks.

The Government has set out plans to restart England's housing market, which has been in deep freeze since the Coronavirus lockdown. From today, estate agents can open, viewings can be carried out and removal firms and conveyancers can restart operations.

Housing Secretary Robert Jenrick said the changes

must be carried out under social distancing and safety rules. It is estimated there are 450,000 buyers and renters with plans on hold.

So, without saying as much, it sounds as if we are returning by default to the strategy of seeking 'herd immunity' once more, allowing the virus to move through the population at will, but keeping the old and the vulnerable in lockdown for some time yet. For nothing has changed as such; we are no closer to finding a way to protect ourselves against the virus. We are letting nature have its way with us, accepting that there will be a second spike, now that our hospital infrastructure is better prepared.

We are stepping out of the dark room, not sure what we will find, but knowing that if Britain is to survive, we have to get its economic engines firing again. It's a tough call. Scotland, Wales and Northern Ireland are staying in lockdown, staying home, looking at what happens in England before making any move of their own. So now we have a two-speed nation.

And what is driving the Government's action to risk a second spike? The BBC offers a story that may well be the reason. The UK economy shrank at the fastest pace since the financial crisis in the first quarter of 2020, as Covid-19 forced the country into lockdown.

The Office for National Statistics said the economy contracted by 2 per cent in the three months to March, following zero growth in the final quarter of 2019. The UK's dominant services sector suffered a record decline. Analysts expect a bigger slump in the second quarter, before the economy starts to recover. This is the first official growth estimate since the UK was put into lockdown at the end of March.

While analysts expected a larger quarterly decline of 2.6 per cent in the first three months of the year, it is still the biggest contraction since the end of 2008, when Lehman Brothers collapsed, the bank that started the global economic implosion 12 years ago.

At the moment, the closely watched R number, the rate of infection, across Britain, is estimated to be between 0.5

and one. But the R number will be much higher in care homes and hospitals, where there are more cases of the disease. Outside those settings, the spread of Covid-19 in the community appears to have been reduced, potentially to below epidemic levels, according to the Office for National Statistics (ONS). This, then, is the gamble the Government is taking, while keeping its hand on the brake, ready to pull hard if things get out of hand, sending us all back into lockdown.

I am reminded of old Western films where a train feels its way gingerly over a damaged trestle bridge hundreds of feet above a river ravine, ready to reverse if the creaking alerts the driver to imminent collapse. It is all down to the driver's judgement. And our driver is Boris Johnson, known as the man with the safest pair of hands in Britain. Ha! Nothing to worry about.

But I do worry, as so many of us do right now about our lives, their meaning and their direction. And I worry about my self-indulgence in writing about my own life. I have been teased a bit by my family about finding my own life the most interesting subject on earth. But who can honestly say that they don't feel the same? Our lives astonish us, as much for our failures as for our successes. We are such gossamer beings, such insubstantial things; if we stop to think about it, our lives and our survival are a constant source of wonder.

The mere fact that any of us live, given the dangers faced over a steeplechase course of millions of years, is a fascination to me. My existence was the cause of outrage on both sides of the family. A Jew and an Afrikaner were not meant to fall in love, get married and have children. My parents lost two children before I arrived, so I have two lost siblings that I know nothing about. My existence (like all of ours) is the matter of purest chance. This is why, I suspect, that I think, now and then: Have I lived enough, achieved enough, made enough out of this priceless gift? Have the curses that heralded my arrival been wrong? I hope so.

Bringing me back sharply to the true subject of this book, Jan sends me two Twitter comments on the issue of the

Government's handling of Covid-19. Radical feminist and domestic violence campaigner @JeanHatchet tweets: "So @NicolaSturgeon has suggested Boris is playing "Russian Roulette" with our lives. I said to Sidekick [her partner], more like legislative genocide. I think it's deliberate. They know who will die. It's the poor, the old and BAME people. All of whom the Tories see as costly rather than human."

And @bencooper replies: "The plan is still herd immunity, it always has been – they just realised they shouldn't say that out loud."

All across England, workers are being encouraged to return to work, and those who have worked throughout this three-month period are fearful. The Guardian describes one man saying: "It is like dancing with the Devil", the two-metre rule impossible to maintain, no protective clothing and maybe just a bottle of hand gel at the washing up sink at work the only nod to the danger.

And in care homes, there is ongoing misery. Care home operators have accused the UK Government of "a complete system failure" over testing for Covid-19 after Government officials repeatedly deflected responsibility for the task and left vulnerable residents unchecked. If we judge a society by the way it cares for its most vulnerable, then Britain is a failed state.

America is not doing much better. Under the headline 'Covid has Exposed America's Most Dangerous Virus', Tim Wise writes in the political magazine *Medium* about racism: "There is a virus ravaging America, but it's not the one you're thinking of. It has been here for a long time, for much longer than Covid-19. It has mutated over time, and some have been struck with more serious symptoms than others, having contracted it. But we have all been exposed, no matter the care we have taken to avoid it. This virus lives in the DNA of the nation, in our history books, our economic policy, our politics. It has roots in our culture and has shaped our worldview. It is a virus so central to America's existence that it is hard to imagine us without it. Whatever antibodies it provides clearly falter.

"It is a virus of indifference to (or active contempt *for*) broad swaths of humanity. It is the same virus we have occasionally located in other lands, while ignoring its presence in our own."

He is of course speaking of racism, which he claims is informing the response to Covid-19 in the USA, and in many other places, doubtless, too.

He says that the US Government, much like the UK Government, is offering us just two options: to stay home (and go broke), or go to work and risk our lives and those of our families. But he says that there is a third option we could take if the stakes were higher: we could force the Government to protect everyone by keeping them safe at home and financially assisted by government. This is not happening, because those that are dying in the greatest numbers just don't matter that much to government or in fact to most US citizens, for a number of reasons. Racism, ageism, classism and ableism.

In other words, we are saying that people of colour matter less (racism), the poor and working-class matter less (classism), the elderly matter less (ageism), and those with a pre-existing health condition matter less (ableism) than our philosophy about the role of the state, even in moments of crisis.

Is this what we have come to? Really?

My mind takes me to a Neanderthal gravesite in northern Europe where anthropologists are studying its remains. The skeleton is that of an old man, his remains surrounded by pollen, indicating the presence of flowers placed in the grave, and that he was clearly loved and cared for, his loss felt deeply. But it is his bones that really tell us most about this society of early man. His one leg has been very badly damaged some years before his death, which would have made hunting and gathering impossible. It is a crippling injury that has healed badly. The fact that he lived on for many years after his injury is clear proof that he was cared for by his community. Are we saying that Neanderthals cared more for the disabled and the old than we do? Covid-19 has shone a horribly clear light on this question. And it seems the answer is yes. God help us all.

And what of the future, how does it look? An article by Naomi Klein headlined: 'How Big Tech Plans to Profit from the Pandemic' is a sobering, long read in *The Guardian*, republished from *The Intercept*, and it casts a pall over my day. The future, it seems, is here already, rushed to us superfast by this pandemic. And this is how the future looks. It will be brought to us by artificial intelligence through the gift of the tech giant companies, which will utterly control our every movement and will invade our homes and our depleted privacy, turning our homes into doctor's waiting rooms, school classrooms, places of work and even prisons, if the Government so wishes. And all of this to supposedly protect us from other germ-bearing humans. The future is going to be contactless. Everything we need or want will be delivered to us, or to those who can afford it. How long will it be before we need a passport to leave not our country but our homes, as trialled in France so successfully?

My own advice is to get outside as fast as you can when it is safe to do so, go travelling, make the most of the old world while it lasts; the new world is going to constrain us, tightly, even as it pretends it is freeing us up. The future is frightening. This pandemic has given us a glimpse of what the future will be. It has also been a reminder of the ultimate lockdown, death, which may come just as suddenly and as unexpectedly as Covid-19 did, changing everything overnight. Don't put off all those things you planned to do. Seize the day and make the most of your life. Remember, we are dancing with the Devil, and who knows when the music will stop.

CHAPTER 40

14th May 2020

Classic car auctions

I wake to a beautiful morning after a bitterly cold night that plunged us to below zero. The frost-silvered roof of the stables and the whitened lawn are a fast-melting memory of just how quickly the temperatures can drop here, even in May.

There is ice on the horse's water buckets and I think how lucky that the man lost on Ashdown Forest is home safe; he would not have done well out for two nights in cold like this. It has been the coldest night in Northern Ireland since 1982 at minus five. But the weather forecast for today in Sussex is good, with rising warmth and the promise of a warm weekend ahead. There is much to be grateful for. I have four days to go to my 70th birthday and I feel well. It will be no small victory to reach it. The trick will be to keep going, to find a way of getting back out there without risking everything.

The news from far-off New Zealand is good; they have lifted the lockdown and barbers report queues around the block for haircuts. Their brilliant Prime Minister, Jacinda Ardern, gets plaudits for the leadership of her country of five million people who've lost just 21 citizens to Covid-19. It may be the country of 'the long white cloud', but there is just a small shadow over the island nation today. So different from our own island nation, struggling to find a way of getting back to life and work safely.

By happy coincidence, I receive a buoyant email from a friend in New Zealand, Drew, a builder by trade, who writes that he and his family are well and that he has managed to keep working throughout the lockdown, fixing up an empty farmhouse for a customer. For years, Drew and his wife Estelle and their children lived here in Crowborough, and he was our 'go-to-guy' when anything went wrong with the cottage. He is one of those wonderful people who can fix anything, do anything. And the cottage still wears the paint he put on it, the plumbing he fixed and a myriad of carpentry jobs.

His mail is the first to bring birthday wishes for me, and I am moved by his remembering. He writes: "All safe and sound down under. Into level two of Covid-19 and the town went mad. Everyone and their dogs came out to play. Shops busy and roads full of cars." He sends news of his family and asks after ours. He is a good man.

By a strange co-incidence, I received another email from New Zealand earlier this week, from a man seeking a Spitfire engine. He read a story of mine for H&H Classics, which sold one of the legendary aircraft engines recently, and he asks if I might help him to source another. I put him in touch with Damian, Head of Sales at H&H Classics, who will be just the man to help him find one. Damian has an encyclopaedic knowledge of the classic car world, which touches on classic boats and planes too. His network is astonishing.

I have been fortunate to have had contact with the endlessly fascinating classic car world since 1987, when I began consulting for Robert Brooks at Christie's Classic Car Department. When interviewing me for the job, he asked how much I knew about classic cars. I paused for a moment thinking, should I tell him the truth or try to pretend that I did know something about cars. Wisely I opted for honesty and admitted that I was a horseman first and last and that I knew nothing about cars. His face fell and I can remember his answer to this day. In a rather frustrated voice that I grew to know so well, he said: "Well that is a great start! Can you tell a story?" It was the beginning of a relationship that lasted for 28 years, only ending in 2015 when he decided to sell Bonhams, the international fine art auction house he expanded hugely and for whom I worked as Director of Press and Marketing for many years. I bear the scars and recall the bouquets to this day.

The first car whose sale I promoted and which still sticks in my mind was the Kellner-bodied, ex-Briggs Cunningham, Bugatti Royale, one of just six in the world, which was sold at the Royal Albert Hall in London after a photo shoot at Pebble Beach in California. This monster car, the length of a London bus, with a dancing elephant on its six-foot-tall bonnet, nearly got stuck in the service entrance to this prestigious sale venue in London, and Jamie Knight, another stalwart of the classic car world and an all-round good egg, managed to jimmy the door lintel off to get the car in, with a quarter of an inch of space on either side. It sold for £5.5 million, in one of the glitziest auctions of 1987. The buyer was a Swedish property tycoon, who had to sell the car later, when his empire collapsed. On the night of the car auction in London, I helped Nick Harley, Thulin's agent, who had bid on his behalf, out of the Royal Albert Hall discreetly, so that he could get back to his hospital bed, as he had recently suffered a heart attack. How he survived the excitements of the auction remains a mystery to me.

More recently, on behalf of Simon Hope, the ebullient Chairman of H&H Classics, I was involved in the deeply satisfying sale of two Ferraris, owned by the late Richard Colton, a 1960 Ferrari 250 GT Short Wheel Base and a 1967 Ferrari 275 GTB/4. The cars were a legacy Richard gifted to the lifeboat service, the RNLI. Simon sold the cars for £10m, the single biggest bequest the RNLI has ever received. The money is being used to build lifeboats, the first of which, a Shannon class boat named the 'Richard & Caroline Colton', is now based just down the road from us in Hastings. By a happy coincidence, this boat in whose creation I played a small part, is more than likely to be the one to come to the aid of our son Dom, his partner Steph and their cat Juno, aboard their sloop, if they ever get into trouble off the Kent or Sussex coasts. God forbid! Strange old world, isn't it? Shakespeare said: "The evil that men do lives after them; The good is oft interred with their bones." But Richard and Caroline Colton's generosity lives on after them, saving lives at sea.

So much for personal history. This country's and the world's history is being written in blood all around me, as I sit here typing. The BBC announces that Covid-19 "may never go away", according to a warning from the World Health Organisation. Speaking at a briefing on Wednesday, WHO Emergencies Director, Dr Mike Ryan, warned against trying to predict when the virus would disappear. He added that even if a vaccine is found, controlling the virus will require a 'massive effort'.

I can't help but wonder if that massive effort will be forthcoming? There are signs that the line against Covid-19 is no longer holding. Young people feel that they are unlikely to die, and are champing at the bit to escape lockdown, slipping away to meet friends and to party as the summer heats up. The police are beginning to struggle, trying to maintain order on the party front. A lassitude has overtaken many older people, ennui has set in as a result of lockdown, and the Covid-19 threat is losing its power to terrify.

It seems that a loss of 60,000 people out of a population of 70 million in the UK is not enough to engender terror or horror. Unlike the Black Death, which at its worst affected virtually every household. The fact that Covid-19 will be around for a long time seems to pass people by. It does not take a genius to predict that when the brake on lockdown is totally removed, there will be an explosion of youthful high spirits, and the effect could have a deadly impact on the older generation. For a group that resented its elders for cutting them off from Europe by voting for Brexit, this may be a harsh revenge.

Almost 300,000 people worldwide are reported to have died from Covid-19, and more than 4.3m cases have been recorded. The United Nations, meanwhile, warns that the pandemic is causing widespread distress and mental ill health – particularly in countries where there is a lack of investment in mental healthcare. The UN is urging governments to make mental health considerations part of their overall response, as the pandemic has caused widespread psychological distress worldwide.

And amid all of this, 'The Donald' continues on his mad masquerade of pretend Presidency. He says he totally disagrees with top US medical advisor Dr Fauci over opening schools. Dr Fauci warned that rushing to reopen schools and the economy could set back the US recovery. One thing you can say about Donald is that he is consistent in his outrageous behaviour.

And now, a personal plea to the American people: please remove Trump from office in November, as it will greatly relieve psychological distress among your allies around the world. And then we can knock this other virus on its head too.

CHAPTER 41
15th May 2020

Hospital visits are halved by a million

The numbers of people attending Accident & Emergency departments at hospitals each day has halved, a medical spokesman reports today. He says the reason is largely fear of picking up the virus. Heart and cancer patients who need to attend for regular check-ups are just not pitching up. There are also admittedly fewer car accidents, as far fewer people are out driving, compared to normal times.

A&E visits in England have fallen to their lowest figure on record, as people stay away during the Covid-19 outbreak. Figures published by NHS England show that 917,000 attendances were recorded in April 2020, down 57 per cent from 2.1 million in the same month last year. The latest number is the lowest for any calendar month since current records began in August 2010. NHS England said the fall was "likely to be a result of the Covid-19 response". So more than one million people, some doubtless in dire need of medical help, have stayed away from hospital.

A BBC London reporter, Sarah Lee, interviews nurse Louise Wigginton, who has been fighting to save the lives of Covid-19 infected patients. She says that it breaks her heart to see people so desperately ill, and at the same time, observe groups of young people outside the hospital where she works, simply ignoring the social distancing rule and meeting in large groups. She says: "We expect another peak. How many more people can we watch die this terrible death? For how many years will I hear the cries of the families saying goodbye over Skype? We can only take so much. We are not heroes; we have no special superpowers to deal with this. And if we fall, who will look after you then?" She pleads for people not to let her and her colleagues' trauma be for nothing.

As if by serendipity, I hear a spokesman for the psychiatric profession call for treatment of frontline NHS staff for post-traumatic stress syndrome [PTSD], a condition often suffered by soldiers on their return from war zones. I hope that Louise hears this too, and gets help for herself; and that her thousands of colleagues are treated too. We do not want them to fall.

I sit in the garden and type like crazy, driven on by fury and by the fact that I will be 70 shortly, and I feel the shadows on my lawn lengthen every day. I so wish to make 70; it has a nice symmetry. However, time is running out for me, whether through Covid-19, or simple wear and tear. I want to finish this book. I want to leave my thoughts on this time for my kids and any future grandkids. It may well prove to be my best attempt to have a last word. So many voices have been silenced, so many. Some of them would surely have agreed with me that their lives were stolen from them as much by political incompetence as by Covid-19.

The strangest thing about this disease and its effect on people is summed up by the frog in the saucepan story. The water warms up so slowly that the frog is more than comfortable until suddenly he is in pain, and then he is dead. That is how it is. They do not see sick and dying people, they know very few people who've been affected. They are at home and comfortable. It is all too easy to be blithely unaware of the danger. All they need to do is to avoid the news. And yet their lives are utterly prescribed, curtailed, limited and even so, although they are patently in the pot in this transformed life, they carry on much the same. People seem little bothered. It's like a phoney war. They hear talk of bombs dropping but haven't seen any. It is bizarre and this response is perhaps the most bizarre part of it.

As I type, I am aware of the lovely scent of the yellow climbing Peace rose that scales the side of the stables. Its hard, bright yellow buds pale in time to a softer butter shade. I planted it with my mother in mind, as the Peace rose was her favourite. So, as I write, I am gently enfolded by a scent that reminds me of my beloved mother. In many ways, she is as present to me and in me as when she was alive, maybe more so. Her wisdom and humour, her irreverence and groundedness, her earthiness, are the things about her that I treasure. And for each of those qualities, I can think of stories that illustrate them. Stories that make me smile. If I have inherited my father's mind, it is perhaps my mother's soul that keeps me going. I can hear her voice as clear as a bell, and her comment on the issue of our time: *"Ag ja ou wereld, wat is jou waarde? Al wat oorbly is stof!"* (Oh yes old world, what is your worth? All that remains is dust!) She would tell me to be humble: *"Wees maar die minste."* (Be prepared to be the lesser one, referencing marriage). And she would quote too, her favourite line from Revelations: *"In die einde van dae, sal jy gesigte sien en droome droom."* (In the end of days, you will see faces and dream dreams). And finally, as though it would cheer me up, she'd say: *"Onkruid vergaan nie."* (You can't kill weeds, referring to me!) I learned some wisdom from her.

My father is here too in spirit, no doubt. How shocked he would be to see me now, at almost 70, grey haired, silver bearded. But his main interest would be a critical view of our current dilemma, and he would say two things I know for certain. He would minimise the threat by saying: "What looks like a mountain now will look like a molehill, looking back." And he would also say, referencing lost jobs and lost opportunities "When one door closes, another opens." And add: *"Aanhou wen!"* (Keeping on keeping on wins the day). These favourite sayings of his have helped me through many dark days, no less now. And he would add in my mother's Afrikaans, referring to our present leadership: *"Trap jy in kak, dan stink jy."* (If you step into shit, then you'll stink).

Well, as a nation, we have sure stepped into *merde* with this lot. And we only have ourselves to blame. We can't say we weren't warned; we had years to observe Boris at work and play. He did not get into Number 10 by mistake, but by a landslide. And noting this fact, my Dad would have used use another Afrikaans expression about that election: *"Die wat nie wil luister nie moet voel!"* (Those who won't listen [to warnings], must learn [by feeling the pain]).

He would consider the actions of the professional politicians who make up the Government and he would add another favourite expression: "God save me from the professionals." Usually referring to lawyers, accountants, doctors, as well as politicians.

My father would want to know what I earned last year and how much the lockdown was costing me. He would want to know what I was making on *Life in a Time of Plague,* and would be shocked to know that no money had changed hands with BizNews, just the opportunity to publicise the book. That would puzzle him greatly.

By the time he was done with his cross-questioning, I would be exhausted. Being right so often does not necessarily endear you to a person. And he was more often right than wrong. I am still a beneficiary of his many shrewd financial decisions.

A short BBC story catches my attention: A group of macaque monkeys in the United States have done well on a new vaccine, recovering after being given the Covid-19 virus, and similar human tests are already underway. Help is at hand, we just have to keep our heads down until they arrive. I hope those monkeys live long and happy lives.

As I walk into the house to make a cup of tea, I notice the marks the virus has left on our home. In the TV room there is a long gun chest in yellowwood, piled high with post for us and for Dom and Steph, decontaminating, and in the kitchen, the hum of the dishwasher is silent and the hand-washed crockery is piled high, and in the toaster down button, there is a wooden spoon stuck to keep the toaster on when needed – the one that caused the fire. Normally, this equipment would have been fixed with one phone call, but for now, that must wait, and we must make and mend and manage as best we can. There are greater challenges to face, but these small markers are a reminder of the invisible rampaging bear outside the house.

It has been a beautiful day. Besides writing, I went to pay Callum a visit as I do each morning, down in his field below the cottage. This morning I found we were out of carrots, so I grabbed a handful of cream crackers for him. He trotted over as usual, swinging his head, but was not too sure about the cream crackers until I mashed one up in my hand and then he got stuck into them with a will. As he ate, I stroked his beautiful muscled neck, the skin like silk, but warm with it. This is a horse that loves being groomed and will drop his head in sheer bliss as the brushes move over him. I look forward to seeing the world once more from between his ears.

When next we set forth out into the woods and the wide reaches of Ashdown Forest, it will be into a new world that we will be riding. But if I am once more astride this horse, the world can send what it wants; we will cope.

CHAPTER 42

15th May 2020

Of dogs and pies, human cruelty and human kindness

Have you noticed that people who sleep on the streets often have a dog with them, usually lying up close against the owner's legs? These are often destitute people, who are close to the edge of starvation; many suffer from mental illness and a variety of physical ills. But this does not stop them looking after their dogs, which are often in a better condition than they are. I can only imagine that they see the dog as a priority, who should eat first before they do. The dog is a friend, a protector, a comforter. They would be bereft and even more vulnerable without their dog.

Yet, here's a thing: the RSPCA has received more than 1,600 reports of abandoned animals since lockdown started here in the UK. That's 40 a day on average in England and Wales, with 56 of the reports coming from Kent, just up the road from us, since March 23. The animal charity has released the figures as part of its emergency appeal, which was launched to help keep its rescue teams on the road during the Covid-19 crisis. Animal rescuers have been designated key workers, but the RSPCA is in need of vital funding to help its frontline staff continue their work. Head of the charity's rescue teams, Dermot Murphy, said: "Although much of the country is on lockdown, sadly, there are still thousands of animals who need our help, including abandoned pets. Many people are finding their pets are a real source of comfort in these anxious times, but it's heartbreaking that some animals are being dumped during this crisis."

He adds: "In most cases, we don't know why pets are abandoned, but it's really important to remind people that there is no evidence to suggest that Covid-19 can be passed from pets to people. There is lots of help and support out there for anyone else struggling to get animal food, with health or behavioural issues, exercising their pets or managing to keep children safe around pets. Please don't be afraid to ask."

Since the lockdown measures were introduced, the RSPCA has responded to more than 27,000 incidents in total, with 1,663 reports of abandoned animals received. It is urging pet owners to make an emergency pet-care plan should they be admitted to hospital with the virus, including placing a poster in the window informing people that their pet is inside.

Coronavirus is corroding the milk of human kindness, and the human-animal bond is breaking, in some instances. We must not judge, we don't know what hell anyone, maybe living alone, is going through, sick with the virus. Maybe they think that abandoning their pet will help it secure a new home. There is just no knowing. What is certain is that Covid-19 is eating at our society like a cancer.

I need to get away from all this misery for a bit and walk down the hill to see Callum. There I meet Saffron, a friend from the stables next door, collecting her daughter Alice's ponies, May and Jack, from the paddock just down from Callum's. She tells me she has been shopping in local farm stalls, and the greedy foodie in me experiences a shiver of food envy. She mentions that they have wonderful organic asparagus, fruit and veg and very good pies.

She uses the word pies a number of times, which is a bit like inviting an alcoholic out for a drink. There is an instant, visceral reaction – hunger, salivation, and I can almost feel myself twitching. She says it a third time: "All kinds of pies; steak, steak & kidney, chicken, vegetarian, they really are wonderful pies. They make them and bake them on the premises."

Hurriedly, breaking into her flow, I say to her that next time she goes down to the Buxted farm shop, I'd be grateful if she'd pick up some pies for me. She kindly agrees. "Steak ones?" she asks, reading my greedy mind. "Steak ones," I reply. Saffron is the source of all sorts of goodies for Callum and the other horses standing alongside Alice's ponies. Over the past year, she has arrived with carrots and swedes and other crunchy vegetables that the horses love. Now I am cashing in on this cornucopia, hoping she won't forget my pies. The steak pies please Saffron! (And sure enough, two days later, there they are with a birthday card, tucked into the post box in our storm porch. What would life be without friends?)

A great friend from Cape Town, the 80-year-old poet, author and lyricist, Barbara Fairhead Coetzee, a kind of guru to me, and a very wise woman, writes about time, the present, beauty and regrets, in a wonderful email just in, that resonates powerfully with me: She writes, "Most of the time, for almost one hundred years now, we have had those tomorrows – as it happens. So we begin to think we can rely on 'time' as an ingredient for our ventures. Now, we know nothing, nothing is certain. No wonder the panic."

As usual, I agree with her. There is nothing that makes God laugh more than listening to people making plans. And yet plan we must.

Barbara is a force of nature who has lived, truly lived, a tempestuous life. She is the mother of six remarkable daughters. And now is married to a poet, writer and musician nearly 40 years younger than her, Jacques Coetzee, who has a remarkable singing voice and a very fine mind. She is the daughter of Pascoe Grenfell, my childhood hero, a former pilot, Squadron Leader of RAF 13th Squadron during WWII and my late father's fishing friend, who taught me how to fish.

In Barbara's own books, she does something remarkable, capturing landscape and, even more difficult, something of that 'Other' just beyond us. This is what speaks loudest to me in her books. We are aware of the fact that we are walking on sacred ground, that the earth and the universe, a star among stars, is a huge presence in our life, and we forget to honour it at our peril.

She adds: "We need to be gentle with each other. I am going to enjoy to the fullest this small glimpse of the world: our garden, which is also looking beautiful in its arid way. We have the tiniest birds ever, coming to find whatever, from the various succulents, and even from the euphorbia, which looks a bit like Moses' Burning Bush. Some Virginia creeper has crept into one of our other creepers – probably some bird dropping – is now a startling red and scarlet. It is stunning. We need rain. Since Digby's departure, the hadedah birds have grown very brave. Cracker is getting too old to chase them, and I just love that wild cry they make.

"What on earth do I think I can do? I suppose the best any of us can do is not to add one extra negative thing to all that is going on. That, in itself, is quite a challenge at the best of times. So I will not surrender hope. I will hold all of what is best in us, with gratitude.

"To have seen, met, been present at, listened to, some of the greatest things we have brought to the world, and indeed, to the world itself, is a gift. To be able to say: "I have walked there. I have breathed in all that beauty. To know that I, and all of us, are part of this magnificent web, which now must do what it has to do, to find a new balance – that is a blessing I hold to.

"I think the one thing that might give me fear right now, would be to look back, and feel that I had not lived to the fullest. With all of it, the 'good' and the 'bad', I can smile at all the hoo-hah that accompanied it. But I have no regrets about even the darkest of it."

This is a woman who will not go gentle into that dark night. She has just emerged from hospital where she went to get the gnawing pain in her knee under control. But she battles on, and her going will doubtless be like a meteor across our skies. She is a phenomenon. To receive her emails is like hearing the call of brass battle trumpets. She gives me courage. *"Courage, mon brave, courage."*

As I write this, I have just had a sandwich and an apple in the garden for lunch, and Gus is beside me, eyeing the core. He is patient; he knows it will be coming his way.

CHAPTER 43

16th May 2020

A brief rewilding of the world

Nature hates a vacuum, and as man has withdrawn from the countryside and large parts of the world's cities because of the threat of Covid-19 infection, the animal world has moved in, almost as fast as the tide racing across Morecambe Bay – at the pace of a swift horse.

With more than half the global population under lockdown due to Covid-19, our cities have become shadows of their former selves. There is an echoing emptiness amid the glass and concrete towers and on the black tarmacked roads and highways. For some animals, it's proving the perfect opportunity to go and explore. Here in the UK, in the Welsh coastal town of Llandudno, wild mountain goats have ventured into the empty streets to see what kind of new foraging is available with humans absent from their town centre.

There is an age-old wish in humans to return to Eden. We see this instinct at its most powerful among those people and communities now choosing to live off-grid, in tents and tepees and log cabins in the woods across the world's most remote areas. Coming on top of Greta Thunberg's dire warning of climate catastrophe, we've had devastating forest fires in Australia, ice melt in the Arctic and now Covid-19.

So are the reports we are getting of the wild returning shyly to our cities a welcome sign that maybe we have not irredeemably poisoned the planet? That somehow, we can still make a deal with the near extinct species? That there is still time for us to find a balance, an accommodation with nature?

But not all of us are wide-eyed survivalists or green idealists. Many of our more cynical brethren have created spoof videos of wild animals returning to cities, so we must be careful of fake news; the 'Second Coming of Nature' is not here yet. The promised apocalypse still threatens. This pandemic has just been a holiday from ourselves, a species temporarily exiting its niche, until it is safe to return to business as usual.

I am all too aware, as I blunder into this subject of nature – botany, ornithology, climate – the normal purlieu of scientists and specialists, not romantics like me, that I need to be wary, to tread carefully; that I must not let the wish become father to the so-called fact.

As I consider the issue of nature rewilding the haunts of humans, I am surrounded by buttercups, daisies and green grass, the wallpaper of my world just now, and overlooked by more shades of green than any one palette has a right to. The trees are now fully clothed with leaf, burdened by a ton each of vegetable matter, capable of a science of its own, each fluttering leaf converting carbon dioxide into oxygen, these generous big-hearted wooden friends of man. It is a green and sunlit upland here, 900 foot above the Sussex coast, catching every breeze off the Atlantic, funnelled up the Channel.

From space, our world looks dramatically healthier than it did three months ago. There are empty cities, deserted roads and air pollution is dramatically lower all over the world. In London, air pollution was down by a staggering 50 per cent as people gave up driving and stayed home. Analysis of Covid-19 deaths show a very significant link between the most polluted areas of Italy, Spain, France and the UK, and deaths from the pandemic. I wonder if this lesson will deliver a cleaner world post-pandemic, our having learned the hard way that a polluted world makes man as vulnerable to illness as any other animal.

The Guardian reports that nature has reclaimed the ancient site of Stonehenge, the 5,000-year-old monument on Salisbury plain in southern England. A family of hares are nesting there now, and deer are nibbling the grass around the standing stones. There is silence among these giants for the first time in many years, and there is no sign of the 1.5 million visitors who tramp around it annually. If those stones have any sense of their own, any instinct for detecting energy, they must be wondering at the sudden quiet, and perhaps sighing with relief.

This World Heritage site was closed to the public in mid-March, along with other ticketed locations run by the charity English Heritage. Its new animal occupants moved in some weeks later. Whether or not the hares will stick around until Stonehenge reopens to the public – planned for early July – is anybody's guess.

But before its official reopening, Stonehenge will, as it has for 5,000 years, be the focus of the Summer Solstice on 20 June. With the site deserted for the first time in years, English Heritage will be livestreaming the event.

Nature must be rejoicing at all this unexpected change, able to breathe easier as a result. There is a significant benefit to asthmatics and COPD sufferers in the improved air quality, and that must be true of every other creature on earth. Truly a case of every cloud having a silver lining.

I felt an urge to visit Callum in his stable this morning before everyone arrived to muck out and feed their horses, to have a private chat to let him know I would soon be returning, God willing. And then, a rare, sweetly hesitant, shy sound stopped me stroking his neck and I simply stood and listened. Transfixed. It was the sound of a cuckoo close by in one of the trees surrounding the stable yard. My other African bird friend, long haul traveller, thief, shyster, murderer, nest emptier, but lovely, oh so lovely. It was not the first cuckoo I have heard this heartbreak spring of 2020, but it was the closest, loudest, clearest. I barely moved, just listened. We've lost over half the cuckoos visiting Britain this last 20 years. They are becoming rare, so this was an equally rare treat.

The cuckoos come to us in early May out of the tropical rainforest of the Congo, the very heart of Africa, one of the last homes of the last of the great apes, the gorilla. Their route to Britain takes them round the bulge of West Africa over river estuaries and minarets, and out over the Straits of Gibraltar, looking down on coasters and yachts, fast drug launches, oil tankers and container ships. And then through Spain, climbing high to cross the Pyrenees into France, past monasteries and lonely wolf-haunted sheep farms, through France, and once more across a salt strait, the Channel, and home, their second home, at last, for the summer. Perhaps this bird had been watching me standing in Callum's stable and compared me to another big ape back in our mutual second home, Africa. This was romance enough, even for me.

The song lasted for about two minutes and then the bird was gone, and as I strolled home for breakfast, I held this sound-diamond in my head, replaying it as I brushed aside the bracken and foxgloves.

In the evening, walking Gus, I spot a small herd of deer at the bottom of the sheep field. I think of deer and antelope as my spirit animal and am always pleased to see them.

Maybe this link with antelope and deer started with the rare sightings of Steenbok antelope on the Cape Flats outside Cape Town where I rode as a boy, still smarting from the hammering I took at school, where I was a very poor pupil. I'd see these animals always grazing singly amid the Port Jackson trees, and their presence was balm to my soul. I knew then that even as I sat trapped in a school desk, beset by a world of worry and failure, these animals were out there, miles from any human habitation, living their lives at peace, silently, quietly, with no need of a Matriculation certificate, or any need to understand the rules of rugby and cricket. I felt they were brothers and sisters, and so they have remained to this day.

At the age of 19, in the Army, doing my national service in the hot hell of Oudtshoorn's veld in South Africa, there would be the occasional distant sighting of an antelope, and I'd know I was not alone; my spirit animal travelled with me, almost invisibly.

And when I reached Ashdown Forest in East Sussex, having fled Africa and made a new home, I found myself surrounded by herds of deer, hundreds of them, in this former royal hunting ground. Roe deer are the only native deer on the Forest. They are strongly territorial, and so can regularly be seen in the same areas.

The Ashdown Forest deer population increased after the great storm of 1987, which restructured a great deal of the woodland, creating grassy glades and open rides. But the most common deer hereabouts are Fallow deer with the odd sighting of a rare Sika or Muntjac deer. Occasionally I spot a white Fallow deer, standing out clearly amid its brown brothers and sisters in the green fields.

These animals have no predators but man, and that largely by accident. Speeding cars take a terrible toll of them and there are signs on Ashdown Forest listing the number of animals killed each year. Now and then we will pass one, newly killed, by the wayside.

In autumn, the deep woods echo to the sound of stags belling. The roar is not that that very different from a lion's roar and grunt. Once again, I find a sound bridge between my African boyhood and my adult life in Britain.

Stags and deer haunt my dreams. And I know I am not alone, even in lockdown isolation.

Chapter 44

16th May 2020

Teachers opt for detention rather than death

This week, the Government got into a scrap with the teachers, who it seems have a distinct reluctance to lay down their lives for their pupils. How unprofessional and downright cowardly is that?

A cartoon shows the way out of this impasse. The time to go back to work will be when every MP is back at Westminster and it's standing room only in the Commons, and not a moment before. The Government and its scientists were not able to reassure the teachers' unions that their members would be safe from picking up the virus from their pupils on June 1, when primary schools are due to start. The aim is to begin with Reception Year, Year One and Year Six classes getting the ball rolling. It will be interesting to see who wins this standoff.

I mean, it's not a big ask, really, is it? It's not as if teachers are being asked to take on a PE class or even coach football. No, it's simply a request to speed up herd immunity. And if some of the teachers fall prey to the Coronavirus crocs in the shallows, so be it. Life must go on and the price of life is death for some. Though preferably not Tory cabinet ministers.

City grandees are getting restive. If work does not start soon, how are dividends going to be paid to the fat cats sitting the pandemic out on their private islands or in their private country estates? It's all a bit of a mess, this lifting of lockdown. It wasn't meant to be like this. Boris had a speech and a slogan, 'Stay Alert'. Well, blow me down, the teachers are not only alert, they are frankly skittish, and are not wearing it. Back to the drawing board, Boris. Your move.

Parents are lining up behind teachers, not Boris. *The Guardian* quotes one parent whose views are shared by many. Rachael Towers, 44, from Stratford-upon-Avon. She says: "There is absolutely no chance I will allow my children, aged four and 16, back to school as early as June, while death toll figures and cases are still fairly high. I'd like them to go back to school, as they're driving me up the wall, but it doesn't feel safe yet. September is the earliest I would consider. I have the ability to work from home, so I understand it's hard for parents that need to go to work. But what is more important than your children's lives?"

And if this was not bad enough, and public insurrection threatens, suddenly a new enemy appears before Boris's appalled eyes. As Shakespeare put it: "When troubles come, they come not single spies, but in battalions." It is Professor Martin Marshall of the Royal College of GPs, speaking on behalf of his members. He asks the Government for a *plan* on how to get out of lockdown by the use of testing. Who should GPs prioritise for testing, and how often should they test, and could they please get the results back faster from the black hole they disappear into? No doubt Boris would like the professor to disappear into a black hole of his own. Prof Marshall and the good doctors are a new awkward squad. Corporal Jones, in the TV comedy *Dad's Army,* comes to mind, speaking of the use of the bayonet: "They don't like it up them. No, sir, they don't like it up them!" Boris sure does not like it up him, but the pandemic is now so far up him that Corporal Jones, I mean Professor Martin, may as well finish the job.

And this is no random professor. His CV is impressive. Martin Marshall is a GP in Newham East London, Professor of Healthcare Improvement at UCL and Programme Director for Primary Care at UCLP Partners. He leads Improvement Science London. He is immediate past Vice Chair (External Affairs) of the Royal College of GPs. Previously, he was Director of R&D at the Health Foundation, Deputy Chief Medical Officer for England, and Director General in the Department of Health, a clinical academic at the University of Manchester, and a Harkness Fellow in Healthcare Policy. He has over 200 publications in the field of quality of care, and in 2005 he was awarded a CBE in the Queen's Birthday Honours for Services to Health Care.

Boris, this man would like some bloody answers and a plan. And yes, that is a very long scalpel in his hand!

The chickens are coming home to roost for Boris. He is facing mounting pressure to launch an independent public inquiry into the disproportionate impact of Covid-19 on black, Asian and minority ethnic (BAME) communities across Britain.

And now a millionaire businessman is launching legal action against the Government after it refused to disclose minutes of the Government's Scientific Advisory Group for Emergencies (SAGE) meetings that informed its decision to impose the Coronavirus lockdown. Simon Dolan, who owns Jota Aviation, said he received an unsatisfactory response to his challenge over the legality of the lockdown two weeks ago. He and his lawyers intend to go to the High Court to seek permission for an urgent judicial review of the background to the lockdown imposed on March 23. He had sought to obtain minutes from meetings of SAGE.

"We are pressing ahead with the case and expect to be heard within the next ten days or so," Dolan said. "I believe it is absolutely crucial in holding the Government to account — they have introduced entirely unprecedented restrictions on basic freedoms, caused the losses of millions of jobs, destroyed businesses, incurred eye-watering amounts of debt, which will take generations to pay back, and yet they refuse to share the basic information they say they rely on to make these devastating decisions."

Boris is now getting a kicking from all sides, from teachers and doctors, two of the most respected professional groups in the country, from parents of school age children, from Black Asian and Minority Ethnic groups, and from a random millionaire with a bone to pick about secrecy versus transparency. I really feel for Boris… well maybe just a teeny-weeny bit, even as I'm laughing. After all, it is one of the Great British myths that 'You don't kick a man when he's down'. Untrue in practice, but much quoted and much be-loved, like the myth of the gentleman, that bolsters our self-image.

The gentleman is one of England's greatest **PR** tools. This nation, which grew fat on wool grown on the land of exiled peasants; of Aztec gold stolen by the Spanish and then stolen from them; on enslaving a good chunk of Africa and then building the cities Bristol and Liverpool and parts of London (the fashionable and mercantile parts) on the pro-ceeds. This is after all a nation which terrorised half the world, painted it pink and called it an Empire. How did the idea of the gentleman come out of this? One of the expressions that most shocked me was when fleeing apartheid South Africa, I arrived on these shores to hear the phrase: "The wogs begin at Calais," enunciated in Old Etonian accents. To me, the gentleman is one who protects the weak and punishes bullies. Someone, somewhere, has misunderstood its mean-ing. Surely?

But let me quote another expression that I had not heard until arriving here: Maybe on defining the meaning of gentleman we just have to 'suck it and see.' Suck what and see what, I've often wondered. The gentleman, it seems to me is a work in progress. Though like all generalities, there are ex-ceptions to be found here and there who really do deserve this description. I number some among my closest friends and even some clients. I will not embarrass them by naming them, for they know who they are. And manners, after all, are an-other defining quality of the gent, something I am still working on myself.

This lockdown has not been all hellish. One of its

greatest joys (for some) has been the delicious languor of waking up to realise there is nothing to stop you going right back to sleep again. So, porpoise-like, you rise into wakefulness and then submerge gently back to sleep, or just doze and then come up for some more misty wakefulness, taking in the quiet, the deep quiet of the countryside, no sound of far-off traffic, no aircraft overhead, no deadlines, no ringing phones. Just peace.

If you are not struggling to breathe, dying in a care home, in hospital or at home, or grieving for a lost loved one, this has been a revelation, a sort of socialist heaven made manifest overnight as the 'money forest' was discovered. Workers stay home and play with their children, subsidised by the Government, on furlough, with time finally to learn how to play the guitar you were given for your 14th birthday. We know it can't last, but it's had its moments that's for sure.

And if Britain is going to the dogs, dogs may yet be our salvation. The BBC reports that sniffer dogs – cocker spaniels and Labradors – are being brought in to screen large numbers of people. They are already being used by the charity Medical Detection Dogs to sniff out odours of certain cancers, malaria and Parkinson's disease.

The first phase of the trial to use dogs against Covid-19 will be led by the London School of Hygiene & Tropical Medicine, along with the charity and Durham University. It has been backed with £500,000 of Government funding. The Innovation Minister, Lord Bethell, said he hoped the dogs could provide 'speedy results' as part of the Government's wider testing strategy.

More than ten years of research gathered by Medical Detection Dogs has shown that dogs can be trained to sniff out the odour of disease at the equivalent dilution of one teaspoon of sugar in two Olympic-sized swimming pools of water. Dr Claire Guest, the charity's co-founder and chief executive, said she was "sure our dogs will be able to find the odour of Covid-19."

On the home front, our next Tesco food delivery arrives with a new toaster – hurrah! Jan disinfects and I pack away, and I only get bollocked once for trying to pack something away that has not been wiped down with disinfectant. We are making progress. I take our old toaster, the one that committed hari-kiri, out to the bins and say a quiet farewell.

CHAPTER 45

17th May 2020

"Events, Dear Boy, Events"

"Events, dear boy, events" was former Prime Minister Harold MacMillan's comment on the unpredictability of politics, and how events can scupper the best-laid plans. In the case of Covid-19, there was no plan, and for that this apology of a Government is culpable. That much is clear when we look closely at a recap of events compiled by the political lobbying organisation TW-IN, based in Tunbridge Wells:

December 31st China alerts WHO to new virus.
January 23rd Study reveals a third of China's patients require intensive care.
January 24th Boris Johnson misses first Cobra meeting.
January 29th Boris Johnson misses second Cobra meeting.
January 31st The NHS declares first ever 'Level 4 critical incident'. Meanwhile, the Government declines to join European scheme to source PPE.
February 5th Boris Johnson misses third Cobra meeting.
February 12th Boris Johnson misses fourth Cobra meeting. Exeter University publishes study warning Coronavirus could infect 45 million people in the UK if left unchallenged.

February 13th Boris Johnson misses conference call with European leaders.

February 14th Boris Johnson goes away on holiday. Aides are told keep Johnson's briefing notes short or he will not read them.

February 18th Johnson misses fifth Cobra meeting.

February 26th Boris Johnson announces 'Herd Immunity' strategy, announcing some people will lose loved ones. Government document is leaked, predicting half a million Brits could die in 'worst-case scenario'.

February 29th Boris Johnson retreats to his country manor. NHS warns of 'PPE shortage nightmare'. Stockpiles have dwindled or expired after years of austerity cuts.

March 2nd Boris Johnson attends his first Cobra meeting, declining another opportunity to join European PPE scheme. Government's own scientists say over half a million Brits could die if virus left unrestrained. Johnson tells country: "We are very, very well prepared."

March 3rd Scientists urge Government to advise public not to shake hands. Boris Johnson brags about shaking hands of Coronavirus patients.

March 4th Government stops providing daily updates on virus following a 70 per cent spike in UK cases. They will later U-turn on this amid accusations they are withholding vital information.

March 5th Boris Johnson tells public to 'wash their hands and business as usual'.

March 7th Boris Johnson joins 82,000 people at Six Nations match.

March 9th After Ireland cancels St Patrick's day parades, the Government says there's 'No Rationale' for cancelling sporting events.

March 10th-13th Cheltenham takes place, more than a quarter of a million people attend.

March 11th 3,000 Atletico Madrid fans fly to Liverpool.

March 12th Boris Johnson states banning events such as Cheltenham will have little effect. The study finds the Government's plan is projected to kill half a million people.

March 13th The FA suspends the Premier League, citing an absence of Government guidance. Britain is invited to join European scheme for joint purchase of ventilators, and refuses. Boris Johnson lifts restrictions of those arriving from Coronavirus hot spots.

March 14th Government is still allowing mass gatherings, as Stereophonics play to 5,000 people in Cardiff.

March 16th Boris Johnson asks Britons not to go to pubs, but allows them to stay open. During a conference call, Johnson jokes that push to build new ventilators should be called 'Operation Last Gasp'.

March 19th Hospital patients with Coronavirus are returned to care homes in a bid to free up hospital space. What follows is a boom of virus cases in care homes.

March 20th The Government states that PPE shortage crisis is 'completely resolved'. Less than two weeks later, the British Medical Association reports an acute shortage in PPE.

March 23rd UK goes into lockdown.

March 26th Boris Johnson is accused of putting 'Brexit over Breathing' by not joining EU ventilator scheme. The Government then state they had not joined the scheme because they had 'missed the email'.

April 1st *The Evening Standard* publishes that just 0.17 per cent of NHS staff have been tested for the virus.

April 3rd The UK death toll overtakes China.

April 5th 17.5 million antibody tests, ordered by the Government and described by Boris Johnson as a 'game changer' are found to be a failure.

April 7th Boris Johnson is moved to intensive care with Coronavirus.

April 16th Flights bring 15,000 people a day into the UK – without virus testing.

April 17th Health Secretary Matt Hancock says: "I would love to be able to wave a magic wand and have PPE fall from the sky." The UK has now missed four opportunities to join the EU's PPE scheme.

April 21st The Government fails to reach its target of face masks for the NHS, as it is revealed manufacturers' offers of help were met with silence. Instead millions of pieces of PPE are being shipped from the UK to Europe.

April 23rd-24th Government announces testing kits for 10 million key workers. Orders run out within minutes as only 5,000 are made available.

April 25th UK death toll from Coronavirus overtakes that of The Blitz.

April 30th Boris Johnson announces the UK has succeeded in avoiding a tragedy that had engulfed other parts of the world – at this point, The UK has the 3rd highest death toll in the world.

May 1st The Government announces it has reached its target of 100,000 tests. They haven't conducted the tests, but posted the testing kits.

May 5th The UK death toll becomes the highest in Europe.

May 10th Boris Johnson lifts restrictions.

There will doubtless be debate about this time in Britain for generations to come. There are those who will seek to exonerate Boris and his cabinet colleagues from any guilt for the number of dead, and there will be others, like me, who wish to see him held to account. It has been a shameful record of hubris following his election victory, leading to an at best laissez faire response to the worst danger Britain has faced since WWII. It is evident to me that Boris is no Churchill. He all but abandoned the country in its hour of need. But all of this will be for others to decide at a public inquiry.

I am hopeful that some profound lessons may have been learned in the midst of this carnage, and that change may be in the offing after the pandemic has passed. If one thing comes out of this mess, it must be a narrowing of the wealth gap. The base of the social pyramid must be rewarded for holding the rest of the pyramid up. Shelf packers and supermarket staff, corner shop owners, delivery drivers, postal workers, security guards, essential shop workers, everyone in the health service. It has become brutally clear that we are indeed a society – however much Margaret Thatcher wished to deny its existence – and hugely reliant on each and every member, especially those who in normal times are least re-garded. A society which does not work to the benefit of all is a society waiting to collapse. And the country needs a Prime Minister that is deserving of respect.

Jan and I have been in lockdown for a total of 75 days thus far. What comes next is in the lap of the gods. But my horse is calling to me, as are the far green reaches of Ash-down Forest. I want to rebuild my fitness and make the most of what time I have left. And one cannot live on one's knees forever. I will have to take my chances of dodging a second, third, or fourth wave of this accursed virus. I will be careful. But what is a life without a little danger? One needs to face one's fears. There is a buzz to that. *"Courage mon brave, courage!"*

Chapter 46

18th May 2020

Birthday celebrations in lockdown

Finally, my birthday is here. I've made it to 70, despite the virus, and I am filled with gratitude, and something like a sense of achievement.

I have packed a fair bit into these seven decades, and I feel blessed. As I wake on this momentous day, I have so many mixed emotions. As ever, there is the feeling of awkwardness brought about by the knowledge that I will be the centre of attention today, and that always makes me nervous. I am grateful for lockdown, as it eliminates any chance of parties or anything of that nature, which would just be embarrassing. And yet to be able to have had some sort of celebration, a meal out with family and friends, would have been good.

But the sun is up, and it is another beautiful day. Has there ever been a spring like it in England in the past 40 years we've called it home? I don't think so; I certainly don't remember anything like this. The good weather has become so good that we now take it for granted, just like we did the Cape Town summers all those many years ago.

Jan brings me coffee, gives me a hug and wishes me happy birthday. I am grateful to have her with me; we have walked a long and winding road together since I met her, aged 18, at the university where I had arrived as an older student. Her presence is the best gift of any I will receive this day. I know that even before I open my presents, which lie in a pile on the bed where she has placed them. We have lived together on three continents, Africa, Europe and North America, and we have created two amazing children who continue to astonish us. She has had much to contend with in our shared life. I have not been the easiest, kindest or most generous of partners. I come with a temper and many other failings, but throughout she has stood by me, even in our darkest times.

We lie in bed, sipping coffee, taking in the day and speaking a little of the past and about this strange day and its Covid-imposed stillness. There is a huge envelope among the presents, and I open it first and am amazed. It is a water colour birthday card of me in all my ancient glory, sitting in my steamer chair, with Callum looking over the stable door behind me at the top of the garden, Gus by my side and my trusty laptop on my knees, looking much as I have looked this past two and a half months while writing this book. Jan asked our friend, the artist Susie Rotberg, to produce this wonderful card, and she has done me proud. I now understand that their 'socially-distanced' walk yesterday with the dogs in the woods was also a handing-over of this spectacular card. The words inside are as beautiful and I am silenced, as ever, reading Jan's words.

And then the stillness is broken. The phone begins to ring, and the texts bearing good wishes pile in. It is like no other birthday I have known. Usually I get calls from close family and a friend or two. This morning, the calls come non-stop from Cape Town, Santa Barbara, Bristol, with videos of siblings and family singing happy birthday, and texts and emails in the dozens.

One, from my daughter Imogen, in lockdown over near Rye with her godmother, brings me particular pleasure – wishing me a happy day and looking forward to another year. I wonder if she has any idea how much it means to me?

I eventually get into the shower and have breakfast sitting in the sunshine in the living room. My presents, a bone china mug for my coffee, hand-painted with the blue agapanthus of my childhood, books and more books, lie all around me, nature and travel and food writing, my favourites. I have the joy of weeks of reading to look forward to. Later, I sit out in the garden and luxuriate in the warmth of the sun and the company of the busy, dancing, swooping swallows. Who needs a celebration, when nature provides this display?

At 11am, Jan waves from the kitchen door, telling me to come down. I walk down the lawn and see Dom and Steph at the front door, loaded down with bags of food and drink and a huge cake box. I feel my throat constrict and my eyes prick with tears, which I hold back as hard as I can. With their help, Jan has orchestrated a truly splendid champagne picnic lunch which, sitting well apart, we enjoy under the Chinese dogwood tree. There is a huge salad to go with smoked salmon in dill, sourdough loaves, warm veggie quiches and fresh buttered asparagus. We eat and talk boats, and there is love and laughter, and I feel blessed, dear God, so blessed.

I am instructed to open another birthday card, this one from Dom, Jan and Steph, which Steph, this multi-talented woman, has illustrated beautifully with travel scenes. It's my real birthday present. Inside, there are words that once more grab at my chest and constrict my throat. I read on through the blur. There is a choice of three gifts laid out within the card. I can choose between a sailing trip from Italy to Greece, a sailing trip up the Caledonian Canal in Scotland, or a trip along the Canal du Midi in a barge, an ambition of mine, long-held but given up on now, as I do not feel fit enough to cope with locks, steering and French challenges. These people know me so well, they are not surprised when I opt for the canal journey in France. Dom and Steph will do everything for us that is needed, managing the boat and the locks. I will be able to relax on deck like the Queen of the Nile. Who could resist?

And so my day passes in chapters of happiness that will

be hard-wired into my memory for as long as it lasts. Today will be a memory I will cherish forever.

And then Jan disappears to get coffee. Minutes later, I'm told to shut my eyes, and I open them to find the biggest birthday cake I have ever seen before me, with 'Happy 70th Birthday Jules' piped on the top. It's from a French patisserie in Brighton, a huge cartwheel of a double sponge filled to bursting with raspberries and cream, and topped with a fresh-glazed raspberry jam compote and seven candles. It is stunning. Enough for 22 servings, they tell me as I start to cut huge slices that will reduce the servings by half. They laugh and we devour it, and have seconds.

Happiness usually creeps up on you, or looking back, you realise you were happy at some point, unaware of it at the time. Today, sitting in the garden, happiness pours down on me like Victoria Falls in flood. We spend the afternoon lazily talking boats and boat journeys.

Dom and Steph leave in the late afternoon. Jan and I doze on the lawn, as this most perfect day draws to a close. And over more drinks Jan says she has one last surprise; she has conjured up a fresh duck from the high street butcher to roast for our dinner. I am so touched. It is my favourite, and is always our festive meal, but both of us are still too full after our long lunch, and we decided to freeze the bird for another time. There are only so many treats you can manage in one day.

I cannot help but contrast my day with the state of the world. We need to try harder to be so much better. We have been given the gift of consciousness which means that, unlike other animals, we know the score. We know we are going to die. We know we are failing the earth. We know we are destroying our world. And so, as we know this, know it consciously, yet do nothing to help ourselves and our world, that is a death sentence written by ourselves. And it means we deserve to die as a species. It seems we have made a conscious decision to choose death, to choose annihilation. As a species, it seems we've opted for suicide. Is it self-hatred? It might very well be. It is a desperately sad thought. But I do not wish to end my day, this precious day, on such a miserable note.

As I collapse into bed, my mind wanders from the day just past to the past itself. This time in lockdown fosters daydreaming. But I've been doing that for seven decades now. It started by taking me out of my school desk in the Cape Town suburb of Newlands, out over the playing fields with their cricket pitches and up the mountain, to look out over the Cape Flats, the Hottentot Holland Mountains and the beaches on either side of the Peninsula, where I spent my time riding or fishing or swimming. This ability to wish myself away from the present became a lifelong habit; and this night, while tied down by Covid-19, it does not take much for my mind to get up out of bed to go walkabout, as the Aborigines like to say.

Inevitably, it takes me to my horse next door. In my mind's eye, it is once more early morning when I brush him down and saddle him up, and soon we are in the green tree tunnel down to the lake and up the hill past Susie and Ed's home, and then out into the open reaches of the forest itself, gorse, bracken, heather and grass, with the signature stands of dark brooding pines on the highest hills of the forest. These pine clumps look like meeting places for witches' covens or druidic ceremonies. Nothing grows beneath them because of the load of pine needles they shed, making the ground beneath infertile. It is dark and cool within the copses on a warm summer's day and cold, dark and windy in winter.

As this is daydreaming, time travel, my horse is on his best behaviour, moving smoothly through his paces as needed, shying at nothing, doing my bidding so as not to upset the flow of my thoughts, a moving meditation. We turn down into Five Hundred Acre Wood of Pooh Bear fame, and I note the lightning-struck beech tree that I think of as family. It is within its shattered trunk at human head height, six foot up, that Jan and I would hide one last special birthday or Christmas present for our children, gifts from Pooh Bear and his friends, Roo, Piglet and the donkey Eeyore. I smile, remembering their delight at sitting on my shoulders to find a gift once again. And I smile too, recalling the philosophical humour at the heart of A.A. Milne's books that kept parents reading, for the umpteenth time, to children also addicted to the stories.

Further on into the wood, there is a circle of giants, beech trees standing in what looks like a century-deep family conversation. And I know now that they are indeed talking; science tells us so. Their root systems and the fungal fibres that bind them together underground are in effect a nervous system, a brain of sorts. A tree among them struck with an axe, or feeling fire, will telegraph the news to its neighbours. There is an intelligence at work.

As Callum and I step softly in among them, they pause their talk and listen. They know we are there, our footfall, some half-ton in weight, has been noted; it can scarcely be missed. And they are quite still, listening, waiting. They have no reason to trust man or horse; both have a history of damaging their kind, so they wait to see if these two, Callum and I, will do what we most do, stand and stare, before moving on to stroke a trunk, marking out the carved hearts and initials with a finger, nibble on bark or grab a mouthful of leaves. They sigh, but perhaps it is only the wind in their highest branches. Or maybe it is an exhalation of breath as they recognise me. After all, I have been coming here for decades. I have laughed here and cried here and prayed among them. They know me. I feel watched, but in a benign way.

I pick up the reins, and the big copper horse strides ever deeper into the wood. I raise a hand to fend off a branch or to pluck a leaf. As we start to move downhill, I collect him, bringing his haunches in under him to make him careful of the ground. I do not want him to slip. We reach the pond, where we like to stop and watch the reflections, and then there is a good leg-stretching gallop up the hill, keeping an eye out for dog walkers all the while. This horse has a ground-eating length of stride like nothing I have ever known. Soon we have crested the hill and I let him blow to catch his breath; his flanks heave but soon settle; he is fit as a fiddle. He knows we are headed home; he has a compass in his head that set itself a month after arriving here, which tells him which direction home lies, wherever we are in the forest. And he knows every path, every fork and every turning, and will take it unswervingly if I give him his head. But he also likes to stop now and then, and just look.

His home-going stride lengthens into an almost running rhythm and I sit deep in the dressage saddle, feel the warmth of his flanks, the silken sway of his mane, the ears that seem to have a life of their own. It is not long before we are on the last hill home, and then the stables come into view. I unsaddle, wash him down, mop his eyes and nose and put him back in his stable after checking his haynet and water.

I open my eyes, and look at the shadows on the ceiling above our bed; I have once more escaped lockdown for an hour, deep in the woods with Callum. It is a trick that never fails. My school taught me well.

I made it to 70! That is no mean achievement. There will be new challenges to face in the days that lie ahead, Covid-19 not least among them. But for now, I let slip the lines and feel the breeze take me out onto a dark sea. Who knows when or how the journey will end, but I will go with it.

EPILOGUE
The Sacred Landscape

In this time of waiting, enforced by Covid-19, there are opportunities to think more deeply about life and its meaning beyond the constraints and demands of the everyday. If we are not thinking now about the meaning of our lives, our world, our future, then we are truly lost.

We are like ants crawling over the face of God, blindly unaware of the sacred nature of our journey. What we have lost in exchange for scientific knowledge and mainstream religious belief systems is a gift beyond price, and the cost to us is to live in a two-dimensional impoverished world, a life largely without savour or magic or wonder. Is it any surprise then, that our young people and our best people are always in search of fulfilment? They know instinctively that they have lost something of value, but what it is, is beyond them. Maybe the ultimate gift of this virus will be to help us to refocus on the profoundly important things.

I do not wish to belittle the great gifts and blessings brought to us by rational scientific research, or for that matter, by the world faiths. Our lives are made immensely more comfortable by both science and religion. But it has not come free; the cost is incalculable.

I am talking of what our ancestors took for granted, a sense of wonder, of magic, of spiritual power that was invested in us and in our physical reality. The landscape was alive for them, inhabited by explicable and inexplicable powers. The rivers sang, the trees whispered and the very stones had stories to tell, if only one would sit in quiet contemplation and listen!

This is not a plea for a return to a world filled with superstition, though that is part of the lost magic; some of its loss is for the good. It is also not a plea for turning our backs on science or technology, or education. These need to be embraced, for in them lie part of our possible salvation. But they are also responsible for the culture of greed, of dominance over the natural world, of taking for granted everything given to us on this earth. Our intellect has poisoned us and our world.

Environmentalism has at its core an understanding that everything is linked, and that we need once more to worship the world, to treat it as sacred, because it is our only real heritage, our inheritance and the basis of life on earth, not only for us but for every living thing now and in the future, if there is to be a future.

There are words for what I am speaking of, it is called Deism or Naturism, and it is usually spoken of with disdain, as the most crude and basic belief systems known to man, the belief that gods live in the rocks and rivers and mountains and seas. And it is just this that I am arguing the case for. We need to stop long enough to come to understand how such a belief enriches everything in our lives. For if the most mundane thing, the most abject material, is filled with spirit, then we have a better understanding of ourselves as sacred animals moving through a sacred landscape. That belief makes it much more difficult to damage or destroy anything.

When I was a boy, growing up at the foot of Table Mountain in Cape Town, it was no great feat of the imagination to see the mountain as holy, sacred, a spiritual place, the home of those who had gone before. In my dreams I circled it flying as freely as a bird, experiencing that most powerful feeling of unassisted flight. No wonder then, that as I played in the woods and streams near my home, I was filled with a sense of wonder, by the presence of an unseen 'Other' that has never entirely left me. It is, I believe, the oldest known truth, that in ways we cannot comprehend, we are not alone. That we are observed, and the good and evil we do is noted. And that help is at hand if only we would ask for it.

When I was ten years old, some friends and I built imaginative city states out of what lay about us, stones, and twigs, and pieces of tile and brick. After some weeks of play, each of us had created a small world. These worlds were linked by 'ships' and 'planes' pulled on a string, vessels that traded with our far-flung civilisations found behind an oak tree, or halfway up the riverbank. I don't know how it was for the other boys, but the game became somehow more real and important to me than my real life. I sensed in our play something of a great truth, which I did not understand. It has something of what a formal ritualised dance in tribal society seeks to make, a sense of the great wheel of life celebrated in the shorthand of the movements of the dance, a unifying spiritual experience, linking the profane to the sacred.

I read widely, and now and again a writer alludes to 'the Other' in some way or other, the experience of various tribal peoples (which led me to study anthropology at university), a presence felt among the troops of the First World War, books about nature and the spirits of the woods, children's books with their magic doors into other worlds.

Among my books were some now discredited writers, Lobsang Rampa, (the pen name of Cyril Henry Hoskin), author of *The Third Eye*, Erich von Däniken, who wrote of the markings on the Andean desert in *Chariots Of the Gods*, Carlos Castenada, whose book *The Teachings of Don Juan: A Yaqui Way of Knowledge* revealed truths that emerge in drug-induced states, and the books by Laurens van der Post about his experience with the Bushmen of the Kalahari, all seemed to touch on the issues that fascinated me, access to a world beyond my understanding.

The fact that these writers have turned out to be unreliable witnesses is of no account. Sometimes the way to a truth is shown by fools, the illiterate, or by the innocence of children. These writers were in their way all seeking to articulate belief systems that spoke of ways and means that were not currently available or fashionable. They tapped into the great human hunger to understand why we are here, to make sense of this world, and in this they showed something true.

Man cannot and does not entirely live by bread alone. We want more. We want to return to Eden, to innocence, to a life lived with meaning in harmony with the universe. And it is for this that I seek.

I read in later years the book *Songlines* by Bruce Chatwin, which reveals how the Australian Aborigines sang their known world into existence. Using song, they created word and melody maps of their world, which allowed them to walk securely down the songlines that offered safe passage in a harsh landscape. They combined the sacred and the profane and honoured their world with their culture. It was all of a piece. The land was their culture and their culture was the land.

The Romans believed that to walk was to effect a cure. There is something in the act of going on a journey, however small, that offers us the opportunity to experience our world and the worlds it disguises. There is a gypsy in all of us. We walked as a species out of Africa and colonised the world. By walking, we took ownership of the earth. In walking lies a sort of redemption, and thus the pilgrimage was born.

To travel is to open up the potential for being opened up. The Muslim is required to make the journey to Mecca at least once in his or her life. It is a spiritual journey of enlightenment, and I wonder whether it is the journey or the experience in Mecca itself which offers the greatest lessons?

Today, we are tethered to our homes as never before; fear of the world keeps us there, as do the warmth, security, TV and computers. For many children and adults, the landscape is *terra incognita*. For many, the world beyond their street or town is an unknown world, and this at a time of the greatest social and geographic mobility man has ever experienced. They live within the blaring noise of our culture and its total lack of contemplation. Silence is sacred. Quakers acknowledge this in their meeting houses. Out of silence and contemplation comes wisdom.

There is a woman in Britain who has had media attention for her writing, her commitment to silence and her removal to the most remote places in the country to seek out the most intense experience of silence available to her. After 20 years as a busy vicar's wife in a noisy world, acclaimed feminist novelist Sara Maitland embarked on a quest for silence, which took her to ever more isolated and northern houses in Northamptonshire, County Durham and, finally, her native Galloway. In *A Book of Silence*, I found some answers and a great deal of solace.

She is a true pilgrim soul, and on her journey into silence experimented with more extreme forms of isolation – Zen meditation, a flotation tank, a week in the Sinai Desert. She defined the particular sort of silence she was after: solitude, with inspiring landscape.

She moved into the silence the better to pray and to contemplate the richness of life. I believe she is on to something profoundly important. The Bible is full of men and women who sought out silence, prayer and contemplation as a means of revelation.

Where is all this taking me? I don't know. Maybe nowhere. But as I grow older, I am in search of something to help me understand my life's journey. I sense that I have missed much, that I am impoverished with the richness of the 20th and 21st Centuries. I would like to get a glimpse of God's face before I pass into the silence of death. I would like to be more than an unthinking ant.

So, even as we are held hostage by Covid-19 and all that implies, I listen to the call of the wild, to the song of birds, the rush of water, the wind in the trees. I stop and look into the gloom of the woods and note the new growth, the slow silent turning of the world. I pick up stones and caress them.

For in doing these things I am honouring the world and healing myself, and giving a chance for the Other to manifest itself. It may take a lifetime, it may never happen, but at least I would not have travelled unaware, blind to what lies about me, to beauty.

A door has to be opened if one is to receive a visitor. All one can do is to wait and listen and be ready by the open door to offer a welcome.

Julian Roup
East Sussex
16th July, 2020

Other titles by BLKDOG Publishing for your consideration:

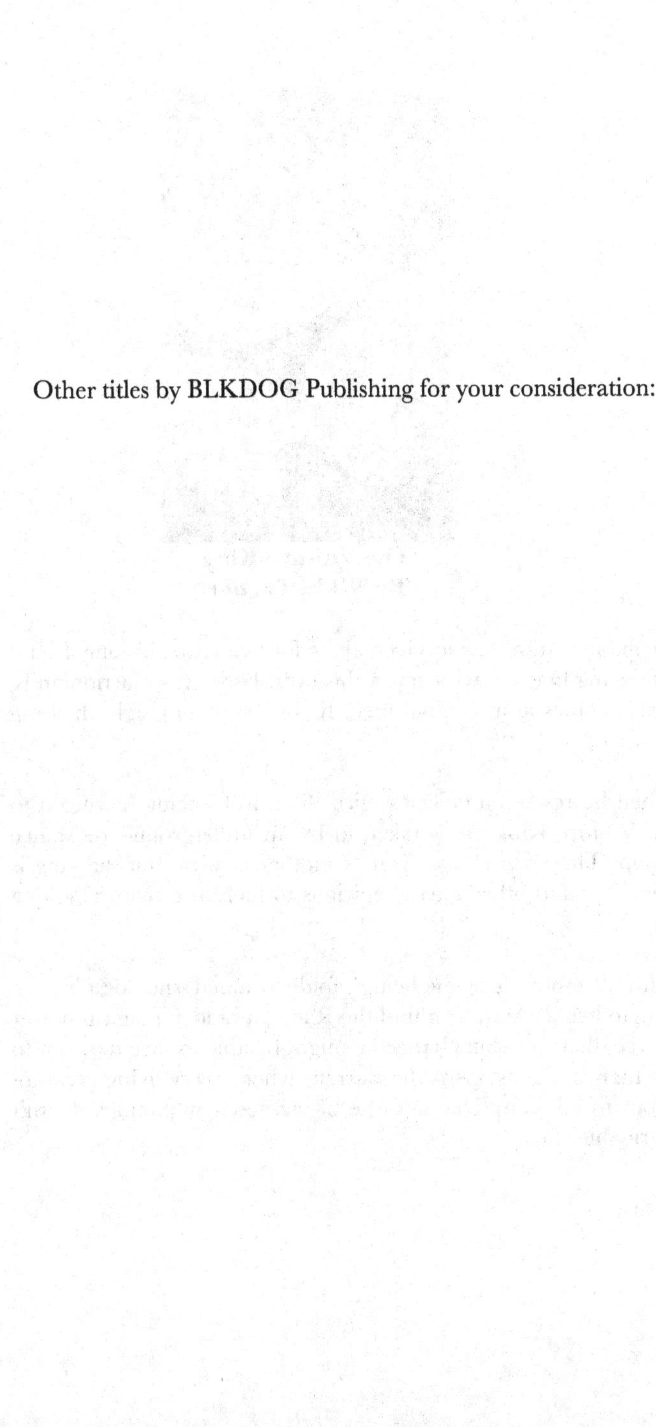

The Vulture King
By Nikki Turner

Orphaned Aram has survived alone for five years, his only friend a thieving magpie, who acts as his eyes. For in the Carrionlands, magic comes at a terrible price. It costs you your sight, hearing or voice.

When he rescues a voiceless girl, Bina, from being sacrificed to the Vulture King, he is taken in by an underground resistance group. They reveal that Aram's mother is alive, but the king is using her and other slave magicians to fuel his unnaturally long life.

With his mother's magic being rapidly drained, she doesn't have long to live. If Aram can find the Radix, a hidden magical power source, there's a slim chance he might be able to save her. But to get there, he must cross the Barrens where every living creature is out to kill you. That's if one of his new companions doesn't betray him first.

Prester John: Africa's Lost King
By Richard Denham

He sits on his jewelled throne on the Horn of Africa in the maps
of the sixteenth century. He can see his whole empire reflected in
a mirror outside his palace. He carries three crosses into battle
and each cross is guarded by one hundred thousand men. He
was with St Thomas in the third century when he set up a Christian church in India. He came like a thunderbolt out of the far
East eight centuries later, to rescue the crusaders clinging on to
Jerusalem. And he was still there when Portuguese explorers
went looking for him in the fifteenth century.

He went by different names. The priest who was also a king was
Ong Khan; he was Genghis Khan; he was Lebna Dengel. Above
all, he was a Christian king who ruled a vast empire full of magical wonders: men with faces in their chests; men with huge,
backward-facing feet; rivers and seas made of sand. His lands lay
next to the earthly Paradise which had once been the Garden of

Was he real? Did he ever exist? This book will take you on a
journey of a lifetime, to worlds that might have been, but never
were. It will take you, if you are brave enough, into the world of
Prester John.

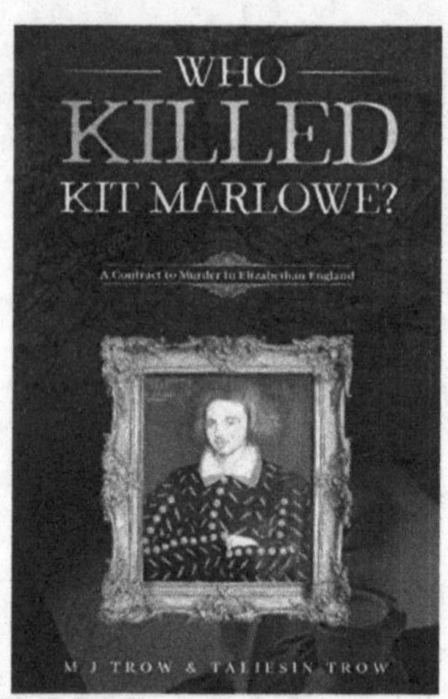

Who Killed Kit Marlowe?: A Contract to Murder in Elizabethan England
By M. J. Trow & Taliesin Trow

Kit Marlowe was the bad boy of Elizabethan drama. His 'mighty line' of iambic pentameter transformed the miracle plays of the Middle Ages into modern drama and he paved the way for Shakespeare and a dozen other greats who stole his metre and his ideas. When he died, stabbed through the eye in what appeared to be a tavern brawl in Deptford in May 1593, he was only 29 and many people believed that he had met his just deserts.

But Marlowe's death was not the result of a brawl. And it did not take place in a tavern. The facts tell a different story, one involving intrigue, espionage, alchemy and the highest in the land.

The brutal murder of a young playwright at the peak of his powers has intrigued and captivated for over 400 years. This compelling journey through the evidence allows us to know, for the first time, who killed him.

Click Bait
By Gillian Philip

A funny joke's a funny joke. Eddie Doolan doesn't think twice about adapting it to fit a tragic local news story and posting it on social media.

It's less of a joke when his drunken post goes viral. It stops being funny altogether when Eddie ends up jobless, friendless and ostracised by the whole town of Langburn. This isn't how he wanted to achieve fame.

Under siege from the press, and facing charges not just for the joke but for a history of abusive behaviour on the internet, Eddie grows increasingly paranoid and desperate. The only people still speaking to him are Crow, a neglected kid who relies on Eddie for food and company, and Sid, the local gamekeeper's granddaughter. It's Sid who offers Eddie a refuge and an understanding ear.

But she also offers him an illegal shotgun - and as Eddie's life spirals downwards, and his efforts at redemption are thwarted at every turn, the gun starts to look like the answer to all his problems.

www.blkdogpublishing.com